Food's Good Side

Cooking with Love

Glenda M. Coulter

1. *To make Elder Vinegar and to colour it.*

Take of your best white Wine Vinegar, and put such a quantity of ripe Elder Berries into it as you shall think fit, in a wide mouth'd Glass, stop it close, and set it in the Sun for about ten days, then pour it out gently into another Glass, and keep it for your use; thus you may make Vinegar of Red Roses, Cowslipps, Gilliflowers, or the like.

2. *To make Metheglin, either Brown or White, but White is best.*

Take what quantity you please of Spring-Water, and make it so strong with Honey that it will bear an Egg, then boil it very well, till a good part be wasted, and put in to it boiling a good quantity of whole Spice, Rosemary, Balm, and other cordial and pleasant Herbs or Flowers.

When it is very well boiled, set it to cool, it being strained from the Herbs, and the Bag of Spices taken out;

When it is almost cold, put in a little Yest, and beat it well, then put it into Vessels when it is quite cold, and also the Bag of Spice, and when it hath stood a few days, bottle it up; if you would have it red, you must put the Honey to strong Ale Wort in stead of Water.

3. *To make Collar'd Beef.*

Take a good Flank of Beef, and lay it in Pump water and Salt, or rather Saltpeter, one day and one night, then take Pepper, Mace, Nutmegs, Ginger, and Cloves, with a little of the Herb called Tarragon, beat your Spice, shred your Tarragon, and mingle these with some Suet beaten small, and strew upon your Beef, and so rowl it up, and tie it hard, and bake it in a pot with Claret Wine and Butter, let the pot be covered close, and something in the pot to keep the Meat down in the Liquor that it may not scorch, set it into the Oven with Houshold bread, and when it is baked, take it out, and let it cool, then hang it up one night in the Chimney before you eat it, and so as long as you please.

Serve it in with Bay Leaves, and eat it with Mustard and Sugar.

4. *To make Almond Puddings with French Rolls or Naples Biskets.*

Take a Quart of Cream, boil it with whole Spice, then take it from the Fire, and put in three Naples Biskets, or one Penny French Roll sliced thin, and cover it up to scald; when it is cold, put in four Ounces of sweet Almonds blanched, and beaten with Rosewater, the Yolks of eight Eggs, and a little Marrow, with as much Sugar as you think fit, and a little Salt;

you may boil it, or bake it, or put it into Skins; if it be boiled or baked, put Sugar on it when you serve it in.

5. *To make Barley Cream.*

Take two Ounces of French Barley, and boil it in several Waters, then take a quart of Cream, and boil it with whole Spice, put in your Barley, and boil them together very well,

Then put in the yolks of six Eggs well beaten, and as much Sugar as you think fit; stir them well over the fire, then poure it out, and when it is cold serve it in; thus you may make Rice Cream, onely do not boil that, but a very little in Milk, before you put it into the Cream.

6. *To make Cheese-cakes.*

Take four Gallons of new Milk, set it with a little Runnet, and when it is come, break it gently, and whey it very well, then take some Manchet, first scalded well in new Milk, let the Milk be thick with it, and while it is hot, put in a quarter of a pound of fresh Butter, and stir it in, when it is cold, mix that and your curd together very well, then put in one Pound and half of plumped Currans, some beaten Spice, a very little Salt, Rosewater, and the yolks of eight Eggs, half a Pint of Cream, and a little Sugar, mix them well together, then make some Paste, with Flower, Butter, the yolk of an Egg and fair water, and roul it out thin, and so bake them in bake-pans, and do not let them stand too long in the Oven.

7. *Another way for Cheese-cakes.*

Take the Curd of four Gallons of new Milk, and put thereto half a pound of Almonds blanched and beaten fine with Rosewater, then put in one Pint of Raw Cream, the yolks of ten Eggs, some beaten Spice, a little Salt, one pound and half of plumped Currans, a little Rosewater, and some Sugar, and so mix them very well, and put them into your Crust and bake them.

8. *Another way for Cheese-cakes.*

Take the Curd of four Gallons of new Milk, beat it well in a Mortar with half a pound of fresh Butter, and then season it as you do the other above-named.

9. *Another way for Cheese-cakes.*

Take the same quantity of Curd, and mix it with half a Pound of Rice boiled tender in Milk, one quarter of a pound of fresh Butter, the yolks of eight Eggs, one Pint of Cream, beaten Spice, two pounds of Currans first plumped, Rosewater and Sugar, and a little Salt, and so bake them, not too much.

10. *To make fresh Cheese.*

Take some very tender Cheese-Curd, stamp it very well in a Mortar with a little Rosewater, wherein whole Spice hath been steeped, then let it stand in a little Cullender about half an hour, then turn it out into your Dish, and serve it to the Table with Cream, Wine, and Sugar.

11. *Another way for a fresh Cheese.*

Take a quart of Cream, and boil in it whole Spice, then stir in the yolks of eight Eggs, and four whites well beaten, and when they are hot, put in so much Sack as will give it a good taste, then stir it over the Fire till it runneth on a Curd, then beat it in a Mortar as the other, and serve it to the Table with Cream and Sugar.

12. *To make Oatmeal Pudding.*

Take Oatmeal beaten fine, put to it some Cream, beaten Spice, Rosewater and Sugar, some Currans, some Marrow, or Beef Suet shred fine, and a little Salt, then Butter your pan and bake it.

13. *Puddings in Balls to stew or to fry.*

Take part of a Leg of Veal, parboil it, and shred it fine with some Beef Suet, then take some Cream, Currans, Spice, Rosewater, Sugar and a little Salt, a little grated Bread, and one handful of Flower, and with the yolks of Eggs make them in Balls, and stew them between two Dishes, with Wine and Butter, or you may make some of them in the shape of Sausages, and fry them in Butter, so serve them to the Table with Sugar strewed over them.

14. *To boil Pigeons.*

Take your largest Pigeons and cut them in halves, wash them and dry them, then boil a little water and Salt with some whole Spice, and a little Faggot of sweet Herbs, then put in your Pigeons and boil them, and when they are enough, take some boiled Parsley shred small, some sweet Butter, Claret Wine, and an Anchovy, heat them together, then put in the yolks of Eggs, and make it thick over the Fire, then put in your Pigeons into a Dish, garnished with pickled Barberries and raw Parsley, and so pour over them your Sawce, and serve it to the Table.

15. *To make an Apple Tansie.*

Take a Quart of Cream, one Manchet grated, the yolks of ten Eggs, and four Whites, a little Salt, some Sugar, and a little Spice, then cut your Apples in round thin slices, and lay them into your Frying-Pan in order, your Batter being hot, when your Apples are fried, pour in your Butter, and fry it on the one side, then turn it on a Pie-Plate and slide it into the Pan again, and fry it, then put it on a Pie-Plate, and squeez the Juice of a Limon over it, and strew on fine Sugar, and serve it so to the Table.

16. *To make a green Tansie to fry, or boil over a Pot.*

Take a Quart of Cream, the yolks of one dozen of Eggs and half, their Whites well beat, mix them together, and put in one Nutmeg grated, then colour it well with the Juice of Spinage, and sweeten it with Sugar; then fry it with Butter as you do the other, and serve it in the same manner; but you must lay thin slices of Limon upon this.

If you will not fry it, then butter a Dish, and pour it therein, and set it upon a Pot of boiling water till it be enough; this is the better and easier way.

Thus you may make Tansies of any other things, as Cowslips, Rasberries, Violets, Marigolds, Gilliflowers, or any such like, and colour them with their Juice; you may use green Wheat instead of Spinage.

17. *To make an Amulet.*

Take twelve Eggs, beat them and strain them, put to them three or four spoonfuls of Cream, then put in a little Salt, and having your frying-pan ready with some Butter very hot, pour it in, and when you have fryed it a little, turn over both the sides into the middle, then turn it on the other side, and when it is fryed, serve it to the table with Verjuice, Butter and Sugar.

18. *To make a Chicken-Pie.*

Make your Paste with cold Cream, Flower, Butter and the yolk of an Egg, roul it very thin, and lay it in your Baking-pan, then lay Butter in the Bottom.

Then lay in your Chickens cut in quarters with some whole Mace, and Nutmeg sliced, with some Marrow, hard Lettuce, Eryngo Root, and Citron Pill, with a few Dates stoned and sliced:

Then lay good store of Butter, Close up your Pie and Bake it:

Then Cut it open, and put in some Wine, Butter, and Sugar with the Yolks of two or three Eggs well beaten together over the fire, till it be thick, so serve it to the Table, and garnish your Dish with some pretty Conceits made in Paste.

19. *To make a Collar of Brawn of a Breast of Pork.*

Take a large Breast of Pork, and bone it, then roul it up, and tie it hard with a Tape, then boil it water and Salt till it be very tender, then make Souce drink for it with small Beer, Water and Salt, and keep it in it:

Serve it to the Table with a Rosemary Branch in the middle of it, and eat it with Mustard.

20. *To souce Veal to eat like Sturgeon.*

Take what part of Veal you like best, and boil it with water and salt, and a bundle of sweet herbs, and a little Limon Pill; when it is boiled enough, put into your Liquor so much Vinegar as will make it tast sharp, and a Limon sliced, and when it is cold, put in your Veal, and when it hath lain four or five days, serve it to the Table with Fennel, and eat it with some Vinegar; you must tie it up as you do Brawn.

21. *To make a Pasty of a Breast of Veal.*

Take half a peck of fine Flower, and two pounds of Butter broken into little bits, one Egg, a little Salt, and as much cold Cream, or Milk as will make it into a Paste; when you have framed your Pasty, lay in your Breast of Veal boned, and seasoned with a little Pepper and Salt, but first you must lay in Butter.

When your Veal is laid in, then put in some large Mace, and a Limon sliced thin, Rind and all, then cover it well with Butter, close it and bake it, and when you serve it in, cut it up while it is very hot, put in some white wine, sugar, the yolks of Eggs, and Butter being first heated over the Fire together; this is very excellent meat.

22. *To make a Pigeon-Pie.*

Make your Paste as for the Pasty, roul it thin, and lay it into your baking-pan, then lay in Butter, then mix Pepper and Salt and Butter together, and fill the bellies of your Pigeons, then lay them in, and put in some large Mace, and little thin slices of Bacon, then cover them with Butter, and close your Pie, and bake it not too much.

23. *To boil a Capon or Hen with Oysters.*

Take either of them, and fill the Belly of it with Oysters, and truss it, then boil it in white Wine, Water, the Liquor of the Oysters, a Blade or two of Mace, a little Pepper whole, and a little Salt; when it is boiled enough, take the Oysters out of the belly, and put them into a Dish, then take some Butter, and some of the Liquor it was boiled in, and two Anchoves with the yolks of Eggs well beaten, heat these together over the fire, and then put your Oysters into it, then garnish your Dish with Limon sliced thin, and some of the Oysters, also some pickled Barberries and raw Parsley, then lay your Capon or Hen in the middle of it, and pour the sauce upon the Breast of it, then lay on sliced Limon and serve it in.

24. *To make an Olio.*

First lay in your Dish a Fricasy made of a Calves-head, with Oisters and Anchovies in it, then lay Marrow-bones round the Dish, within them lay Pigeons boiled round the Dish, and thin slices of Bacon, lay in the middle upon your Fricasy a powdred Goose boiled, then lay some sweet-breads of Veal fryed, and balls of Sawsage-meat here and there, with some Scotch Collops of Veal or of Mutton: Garnish your Dish with Limon or Orange and some toasts for the Marrow so serve it in.

25. *To make Cracknels.*

Take half a Pound of fine Flower, and as much fine Sugar, a few Coriander seeds bruised, and some Butter rubbed into the Flower, wet it with Eggs, Rosewater and Cream, make it into a Paste, and rowl it in thin Cakes, then prick them and bake them; then wash them over with Egg and a little Rosewater, then dry them again in the Oven to make them crisp.

26. *To make good Sauce for a boiled Leg of Mutton.*

Take the best Prunes and stew them well with white Wine or Claret, and some whole Spice, then drain them into a Dish and set it over a Chafing dish of Coles; put to it a little grated Bread, juice of Limon and a little salt, then lay your Mutton in a Dish, being well boiled with water and salt, pour your sauce to it:

Garnish your Dish with Limon, Barberries, Parsly, and so serve it in.

27. *To rost Pork without the Skin.*

Take any joint of small Pork, not salted and lay it to the fire till the Skin may be taken off, then take it from the fire and take off the Skin, then stick it with Rosemary and Cloves, and lay it to the fire again, then salt it and rost it carefully, then make Sauce for it with Claret Wine, white bread sliced thin, a little water, and some beaten Cinamon; boil these well together, then put in some Salt, a little Butter, Vinegar, or Juice of Limon, and a little sugar, when your Pork is rosted enough, then flower it, and lay it into a Dish with the Sauce, and serve it in.

28. *To roste a Pig like Lamb.*

Take a Pig—cut it in quarters, and truss it like quarters of Lamb, then spit it, and rost it till you may take off the Skin, then take the Spit from the fire, and take the skin clean off, then draw it with Parsly, and lay it to the fire, baste it with Butter, and when it is enough, flower it and serve it to the Table with Butter, the Juice of Orange, and gross Pepper, and a little Salt.

41. *To make a Pie with Eels and Oisters.*

Make your Paste, and roul it thin, and lay it into your baking Pan, then take great Eels and flay them, and gut them, cut them in pieces, and wash them, and dry them, then lay some Butter into your Pie, and season your Eels with Pepper, Salt, Nutmeg, Cloves and Mace, and lay them in, then cover them all over with greast Oisters, and put in three or four Bay Leaves, then put in more of your beaten Spices and Salt, then cover them well with Butter, and put in two or three Spoonfuls of white Wine, so close it and bake it, then serve it in hot to the Table.

42. *To make a Pie with Parsneps and Oisters very good.*

Take your Parsneps tenderly boiled; and slice them thin, then having your Paste ready laid in your baking-pan, put in a good store of Butter, then lay in a Lay of Parsneps, and some large Mace, and Pepper cracked, then some Oisters and Yolks of Eggs hard boiled, then more Spice and butter, then more Parsneps, then more Oisters, then more hard Eggs, more Spice, and cover it well, and bake it, and serve it in hot.

Take your largest Cucumbers, and wash them and put them into boiling water made quick with Salt, then when they are boiled enough, take them and peel them and break them into a Cullender, and when the Water is well drained from them, put them into a hot Dish, and pour over them some Butter and Vinegar a little Pepper and Salt, strew Salt on your Dish brims, lay some of the Rind of them about the Dish cut in several Fancies, and so serve them to the Table.

45. *To make several Sallads, and all very good.*

Take either the stalks of Mallows, or Turnip stalks when they run to seed, or stalks of the herb Mercury with the seedy head, either of these while they are tender put into boiling Water and Salt, and boiled tender, and then Butter and Vinegar over them.

46. *To make a Sallad of Burdock, good for the Stone, another of the tender stalks of Sow-thistles.*

Take the inside of the Stalks of Burdock, and cut them in thin slices, and lay them in water one whole day, shifting them sometimes, then boil them, and butter them as you do the forenamed.

Also the tender Stalks of Sow-thistles done in like manner, are very good and wholsome.

47. *To make a Tart of Spinage.*

Take a good quantity of green Spinage, boil it in water and salt, and drain it well in a Cullender, then put to it plumped Currans, Nutmeg, Salt, Sugar and Butter, with a little Cream, and the yolks of hard Eggs beaten fine, then having your Paste ready laid in your baking-pan, lay in a little butter, and then your Spinage, and then a little Butter again; so close it, and bake it, and serve it to the Table hot, with Sugar strewed over it.

48. *Artichoke Cream.*

Take the tender bottoms of Artichokes, and beat them in a Mortar, and pick out all the strings, then boil a quart of Cream with large Mace and Nutmeg, then put in your bottoms, and when they have boiled a while, put in the yolks of six Eggs well beaten, and so much Sugar as you think fit, and heat them together over the fire, then pour it into a Dish, and when it is cold serve it in with Sugar strewed over it.

49. *To make very fine Rolls for Noble Tables.*

Take half a Peck of fine Flower, the yolks of 4 Eggs and a little Salt, with a Pint of Ale yest, mix them together, and make them into a Paste with warm Milk and a little Sack, them mould it well, and put it into a warm Cloth to rise, when your Oven is hot, mould it again, and make it into little Rolls, and bake them, then rasp them, and put them into the Oven again for a while, and they will eat very crisp and fine.

50. *To make short Rolls.*

Take half a peck of fine Flower, and break into it one pound and half of fresh Butter very small, then bruised Coriander seeds, and beaten Spice with a very little Salt and some Sugar, and a Pint of Ale-yest, mix them well together, and make them into a Paste with warm Milk and Sack:

Then lay into it a warm Cloth to rise, and when your Oven is hot, make it into Rolls, and prick them, and bake them, and when they are baked, draw them and cover them till they be cold; these also eat very finely, if you butter some of them while they are hot.

51. *To dress Soals a fine way.*

Take one pair of your largest Soals, and flay them on both sides, then fry them in sweet Suet tried up with Spice, Bay leaves, and Salt, then lay them into a Dish, and put into them some Butter, Claret Wine and two Anchovies, cover them with another Dish, and set them over a Chafingdish of Coals, and let them stew a while, then serve them to the Table, garnish your Dish with Orange or Limon, and squeeze some over them.

52. *To stew Fish in the Oven.*

Take Soals, Whitings or Flounders, and put them into a Stew-pan with so much water as will cover them, with a little Spice and Salt, a little white Wine or Claret, some Butter, two Anchovies, and a bundle of sweet herbs, cover them and set them into an Oven not too hot; when they are enough, serve them in; Garnish your Dish wherein they lie with Barberries, raw Parsley, and slices of Limon, and lay Sippets in the bottom.

53. *To bake Collops of Bacon and Eggs.*

Take a Dish and lay a Pie-plate therein, then lay in your Collops of Bacon, and break your Eggs upon them.

Then lay on Parsley, and set them into an Oven not too hot, and they will be rather better than fried.

54. *To make Furmity.*

Take some new Milk or Cream, and boil it with whole Spice, then put in your Wheat or Pearl Barley boiled very tender in several Waters, when it hath boiled a while, thicken it with the yolks of Eggs well beaten, and sweeten it with Sugar, then serve it in with fine Sugar on the Brims of the Dish.

55. *To make Barly Broth.*

Take French Barley boiled in several waters, and to a Pound of it, put three quarts of water, boil them together a while with some whole Spice, then put in as many Raisins of the Sun and Currans as you think fit, when it is well boiled, put in Rosewater, Butter and Sugar, and so eat it.

56. *To make Barley Broth with Meat.*

Take a Knuckle of Veal, and the Crag-end of a Neck of Mutton, and boil them in water and salt, then put in some Barly, and whole Spice, and boil them very well together, then put in Raisins stoned, and Currans, and a few Dates stoned and sliced thin; when it is almost enough, put in some Cream, and boil it a while, then put in plumped Prunes, and the yolks of Eggs, Rosewater and Sugar, and a little Sack, so serve it in; Garnsh your Dish with some of the Raisins and Prunes and fine Sugar; this is very good and nourishing for sick or weak people.

57. *To make Furmity with Meat-Broth.*

Boil a Leg of Beef in water and salt, and put in a little whole Spice; when it is boiled tender; take it up, and put into the Broth some Wheat ready boiled, such as they sell in the Market, and when that hath boiled a while, put in some Milk, and let that boil a while, then thicken it with a little Flower, or the yolks of Eggs, then sweeten it with Sugar, and eat it.

58. *To make Furmity with Almonds.*

Take three Quarts of Cream, and boil it with whole Spice, then put in some pearled Barley first boiled in several waters, and when they have boiled together a while, then put in so many blanched Almonds beaten fine with Rosewater, as you think may be enough, about four Ounces of Barly to this quantity of Cream will be enough, and four Ounces of Almonds, boil them well together, and sweeten it with Sugar, and so serve it in, or eat it by the way, you may put in Saffron if you please.

59. *To make a hasty Pudding.*

Take one quart of Cream and boil it, then put in two Manchets grated, and one pound almost of Currans plumped, a little Salt, Nutmeg and Sugar, and a little Rosewater, and so let them boil together, stirring them continually over the Fire, till you see the butter arise from the Cream, and then pour it into a Dish and serve it in with fine Sugar strewed on the brims of the Dish.

60. *Another way to make a hasty Pudding.*

Take good new milk and boil it, then put in Flower, plumped Currans, beaten spice, Salt and Sugar, and stir it continually till you find it be enough, then serve it in with Butter and Sugar, and a little Wine if you please.

61. *To make Spanish Pap.*

Boil a quart of Cream with a little whole Spice, when it is well boiled, take out the Spice, and thicken it with Rice Flower, and when it is well boiled, put in the yolks of Eggs, and Sugar and Rosewater, with a very little Salt, so serve it to the Table either hot or cold, with fine Sugar strewed on the brims of the Dish.

62. *To make Gravie Broth.*

Take a good fleshy piece of Beef, not fat, and lay it down to the fire, and when it begins to rost, slash it with a Knife to let the Gravie run out, and continually bast it with what drops from it and Claret Wine mixed together, and continually cut it, and bast it till all the Gravie be out, then take this Gravie and set it over a Chafingdish of Coals with some whole Spice, Limon Pill, and a little Salt, when you think it is enough, lay some Sippets into another Dish, and pour it in, and serve it to the Table; Garnish your Dish with Limon and Orange; if you please you may leave out the Sippets and put in some poach'd Eggs, done carefully.

63. *To make French Pottage.*

Take an equal quantity of Chervil, hard Lettice and Sorrel, or any other Herb as you like best, in all as much as a Peck will hold pressed down, pick them well, and wash them, and drain them from the water, then put them into a Pot with half a pound of fresh Butter, and set them over the fire, and as the Butter melts, stir them down in it till they are all within the Butter, then put some water in, and a Crust of bread, with some whole Cloves and a little Salt, and when it is well boiled, take out the Crust of bread, and put in the yolks of four Eggs well beaten, and stir them together over the fire, then lay some thin slices of white bread into a deep dish, and pour it in.

64. *To make Cabbage Pottage.*

Take a Leg of Beef and a Neck of Mutton, and boil them well in water and salt, then put in good store of Cabbage cut small, and some whole Spice, and when it is boiled enough, serve it in.

65. *To make a Sallad of cold meat.*

Take the brawn of a cold Capon, or a piece of cold Veal, and mince it very small, with some Limon pill, then put in some Oil, Vinegar, Capers, Caviare, and some Anchovies, and mix them very well, then lay it in a Dish in the form of a Star, and serve it in; Garnish your Dish with Anchovies, Limon and Capers.

66. *To dry a Goose.*

Take a fair fat Goose, and powder it about a Month or thereabouts, then hang it up in a Chimney as you do Bacon, and when it is throughly dry, boil it well and serve it to the Table with some Mustard and Sugar, Garnish your Dish with Bay leaves: Hogs Cheeks are very good dried thus.

67. *To dress Sheeps Tongues with Oysters.*

Take your Sheeps Tongues about six of them, and boil them in water and salt till they be tender, then peel them, and slice them thin, then put them into a Dish with a quart of great Oisters; a little Claret wine and some whole Spice, let them stew together a while, then put in some Butter and the yolks of three Eggs well beaten, shake them well together, then lay some Sippets into a Dish, and put your Tongues upon them; Garnish your Dish with Oisters, Barberries, and raw Parsley, and serve it in.

68. *To make a Neats-tongue Pie.*

Let two small Neats tongues or one great one be tenderly boiled, then peel them and slice them very thin, season them with Pepper and Salt, and Nutmeg; then having your Paste ready laid into your baking-pan, lay some Butter in the bottom, then lay in your Tongues, and one pound of Raisins of the Sun, with a very little Sugar, then lay in more butter, so close it and bake it, then cut it up, and put in the yolks of three Eggs, a little Claret Wine and Butter, stir it well together, and lay on the Cover, and serve it; you may add a little Sugar if you please.

69. *A Capon with white Broth.*

Take a large Capon, and draw him, and truss him, and boil him in water and a little salt, with some whole Spice:

When you think it is almost enough, put in one pound of Currans well washed and picked, four Ounces of Dates stoned and diced thin, and when they have boiled enough, put in half a pound of sweet Almonds blanched and beaten fine with Rose-water, strain them in with some of the Liquor, then put in some Sack and Sugar; then lay some thin slices of white bread into a deep Dish, and lay your Capon in the midst, then pour your Broth over it.

Garnish your dish with plumped Raisins and Prunes, and serve it in.

70. *To make a Calvesfoot Pie.*

Take six Calves feet tenderly boiled, and cut them in halves, then make some Paste with fine Flower, Butter, cold Cream and the yolk and white of one Egg, rowl it very thin, and lay it into your baking-pan, then lay some butter in the bottom, and then your Calves feet with some large Mace, half a pound of Raisins of the Sun, half a pound of Currans, then lay more butter and close it and bake it, then cut it up, and put in the yolks of three Eggs, some white Wine, Butter and a little Salt, and so serve it to the Table; Garnish your Dish with pretty Conceits made in Paste, and baked a little.

71. *To make an Artichoke Pie.*

Make your Paste as before named, and roul it thin, and lay it into your baking-pan.

Then lay in Butter sliced thin, and then your bottoms of Artichokes tenderly boiled, season it with a little Salt, a little gross Pepper, and some sliced Nutmeg, with a blade or two of Mace and a little Sugar, then lay in some Marrow, Candied Orange and Citron Pill, with some Candied Eringo Roots; then cover it with butter, and close it with your Paste, and so bake it, then cut it up, and put in white Wine, Butter, and the yolks of Eggs and Sugar; cover it again, and serve it to the Table.

72. *To make an Oyster-Pie.*

Make your Paste as before, and lay it in your Pan, then lay in Butter, and then put in as many great Oysters as will almost fill your Pan, with their Liquor strained, some whole Pepper, Mace and Nutmeg; then lay in Marrow and the Yolks of hard Eggs, so cover them with Butter, close them, and bake your Pie, then put in White Wine, Anchovies, Butter and the Yolks of Eggs; cover it again and serve it the Table.

73. *To make a Pig-Pie.*

Take a large Pig and slit it in two, and bone it, onely the two sides, not the head, then having your Paste ready laid in your Pan, and some Butter in the bottom, lay in your Pig, season it with Pepper, Salt, Nutmeg and Mace, and one handful of Sage shred small and mixed with the Spice and Salt, then lay in more Butter, close it, and bake it.

Serve it in cold with Mustard, and garnish your Dish with Bay Leaves.

If you would eat it hot, you must leave out the Pepper and some of the Salt, and put in store of Currans, and when it comes out of the Oven, put in some Butter, Vinegar, and Sugar, and so serve it.

74. *To make a Rasberry Tart.*

Take some Puff-paste rolled thin, and lay it into your Baking-Pan, then lay in your Rasberries and cover them with fine Sugar, then close your Tart and bake it; then cut it up, and put in half a Pint of Cream, the yolks of two or three Eggs well beaten, and a little Sugar; then serve it in cold with the Lid off, and sugar strewed upon the brims of the Dish.

75. *To make a Carp Pie.*

Have your Paste ready laid in your bake-pan, and some Butter in the bottom.

Then take a large Carp, scale him, gut him, and wash him clean, and dry him in a Cloth, then lay him into your Pan with some whole Cloves, Mace, and sliced Nutmeg, with two handfuls of Capers, then put in some White Wine, and mix some Butter with Salt, and lay all over; then close it, and bake it; this is very good to be eaten either hot or cold.

76. *To boil a Goose or Rabbits with Sausages.*

Take a large Goose a little powdered, and boil it very well, or a couple of Rabbits trussed finely; when either of these are almost boiled, put in a Pound of Sausages, and boil them with them, then lay either of these into a Dish, and the Sausages here and there one, with some thin Collops of Bacon fryed, then make for Sauce, Mustard and Butter, and so serve it in.

77. *To make a Fricasie of Veal, Chicken, or Rabbits, or of any thing else.*

Take either of these and cut them into small pieces, then put them into a frying pan with so much water as will cover them with a little salt, whole Spice, Limon Pill and a bundle of sweet herbs, let them boil together till the Meat be tender, then put in some Oysters, and when they are plumped, take a little Wine, either White or Claret, and two Anchovies dissolved therein with some Butter, and put all these to the rest, and when you think your Meat is enough, take it out with a little Skimmer, and put it into a Dish upon Sippets; then put into your Liquor the yolks of Eggs well beaten, and mix them over the fire, then pour it all over your Meat; Garnish your Dish with Barberries, and serve it in; this Dish you may make of raw meat or of cold meat which hath been left at Meals.

78. *To make Scotch Collops of Veal or Mutton.*

Take your meat and slice it very thin, and beat it with a rolling-pin, then hack it all over, and on both sides with the back of a Knife, then fry it with a little Gravie of any Meat, then lay your Scotch Collops into a Dish over a Chafingdish of Coals, and dissolve two Anchovies in Claret Wine, and add to it some butter and the yolks of three Eggs well beaten, heat them together, and pour it over them:

Then lay in some thin Collops of Bacon fryed, some Sausage meat fried, and the yolks of hard Eggs fryed after they are boiled, because they shall look round and brown, so serve it to the Table.

79. *To make a Pudding of a Manchet.*

Take a Manchet, put it into a Posnet, and fill the Posnet up with Cream, then put in Sugar and whole Spice, and let it boil leisurely till all the Cream be wasted away, then put it into a Dish, and take some Rosewater, and Butter and Sugar, and pour over it, so serve it in with fine Sugar strewed all over it.

Your Manchet must be chipped before you put it into the Cream.

80. *To make a Calves head Pie.*

Make your Paste, and lay it into your Pan as before, then lay in Butter, and then your Calves Head, being tenderly boiled, and cut in little thin bits, and seasoned with Pepper, Salt and Nutmeg, then put in some Oysters, Anchovies and Claret Wine, with some yolks of hard Eggs and Marrow, then cover it with Butter, and close it and bake it; when it is baked, eat it hot.

81. *To dry Tongues.*

Take some Pump water and Bay salt, or rather refined Saltpeter, which is better; make a strong Brine therewith, and when the Salt is well melted in it, put in your Tongues, and let them lie one Week, then put them into a new Brine, made in the same manner, and in that let them lie a week longer, then take them out, and dry-salt them with Bay Salt beaten small, till they are as hard as may be, then hang them in the Chimney where you burn Wood, till they are very dry, and you may keep them as long as you please; when you would eat of them, boil them with [Transcriber's note: word missing] in the Pot as well as Water, for that will make them look black, and eat tender, and look red within; when they are cold, serve them in with Mustard and Sugar.

82. *To make Angelot Cheese.*

Take some new Milk and strokings together, the quantity of a Pail full, put some Runnet into it, and stir it well about, and cover it till your Cheese be come, then have ready narrow deep Moats open at both ends, and with your flitting Dish fill your Moats as they stand upon a board, without breaking or wheying the Cheese, and as they sink, still fill them up, and when you see you can turn them, which will be about the next day, keep them with due turning twice in a day, and dry them carefully, and when they are half a year old, they will be fit to be eat.

83. *To make a Hare-Pie.*

Take the flesh of a very large Hare, and beat it in a Mortar with as much Marrow or Beef Suet as the Hare contains, then put in Pepper, Salt, Nutmeg, Cloves and Mace, as much as you judge to be fit, and beat it again till you find they be well mixed, then having your Paste ready in your

Baking-Pan, lay in some Butter, and then your Meat, and then Butter again; so close it, and bake it, and when it is cold, serve it in with Mustard and Sugar, and garnish your Dish with Bay leaves; this will keep much longer than any other Pie.

84. *To rost a Shoulder of Venison or of Mutton in Bloud.*

Take the Bloud of either the Deer or the Sheep, and strain it, and put therein some grated Bread and Salt, and some Thyme plucked from the Stalks, then wrap your Meat in it and rost it, and when you see the bloud to be dry upon it, baste it well with butter, and make sauce for it with Claret Wine, Crums of Bread and Sugar, with some beaten Cinamon, salt it a little in the rosting, but not too much; you may stick it with Rosemary if you will.

85. *To stew a Pig.*

Lay a large Pig to the Fire, and when it is hot, skin it, and cut it into divers pieces, then take some white wine and strong broth, and stew it therein with an Onion or two cut very small, a little Pepper, Salt, Nutmeg, Thyme, and Anchovies, with some Elder Vinegar, sweet Butter and Gravie; when it is enough, lay Sippets of French Bread in your Dish, and put your Meat thereon.

Garnish your Dish with Oranges and Limons.

86. *To make a Fricasie of Sheeps feet.*

Take your Sheeps feet tenderly boiled, and slit them, and take out the knot of hair within, then put them into a Frying-pan with as much water as will cover them, a little Salt, Nutmeg, a blade of Mace, and a bundle of sweet herbs, and some plumped Currans; when they are enough, put in some Butter, and shake them well together, then lay Sippets into a Dish, and put them upon them with a Skimmer, then put into your Liquor a little Vinegar, the yolks of two or three Eggs, and heat it over the fire, and pour it over them; Garnish your Dish with Barberries, and serve it to the Table.

87. *To make a Steak-Pie with Puddings in it.*

Lay your Paste ready in your Pan, and lay some butter in the bottom, then lay a Neck of Mutton cut into steaks thereon, then take some of the best of a Leg of Mutton minced small, with as much Beef Suet as Mutton; season it with beaten Spice and Salt, and a little Wine, Apples shred small, a little Limon Pill, a little Verjuice and Sugar, then put in some Currans, and when they are well mixed, make it into Balls with the yolks of Eggs, and lay them upon the steaks, then put in some Butter and close your Pie and bake it, and serve it in hot.

88. *To dress Salmon or other Fish by Infusion, a very good way.*

Take a Joul of Salmon, or a Tail, or any other part, or any other Fish which you like, put it into a Pot or Pan, with some Vinegar, Water and Salt, Spice, sweet herbs, and white Wine; when it is enough, lay it into a Dish, and take some of the Liquor with an Anchovie or two, a little Butter and the yolks of Eggs beaten; heat these over the fire, and poure over your Fish; if you please, you may put in shrimps, but then you must put in the more Butter; Garnish your Dish with some Limon or Orange, and some Shrimps.

89. *To make Loaves to Butter.*

Take the yolks of twelve Eggs, and six Whites, a little Yeast, Salt and beaten Ginger, wet some Flower with this, and make it into a Paste, let it lie to rise a while, and then make it into Loaves, and prick them, and bake them, then put in white wine and butter and sugar, and serve it in.

90. *To make a Calves Chaldron Pie, and Puddings also of it.*

Take a fat Calves Chaldron boiled tender, and shred it very small, then season it with beaten spice and salt:

Then put in a pound of Currans and somewhat more, and as much Sugar as you think fit, and a little Rosewater; then having your Pie ready, fill it with this, and press it down; close it and bake it, then put some Wine into it, and so eat it.

If you will make Puddings of it, you must add a little Cream and grated bread, a little Sack, more Sugar, and the yolks of Eggs, and so you may bake them, or boil, or fry them.

91. *To make Rice-Cream.*

Boil a quart of Cream, then put in two handfuls of Rice Flower, and a little fine Flower, as much Sugar as is fit, the yolk of an Egg, and some Rosewater.

92. *To make a Pompion-Pie.*

Having your Paste ready in your Pan, put in your Pompion pared and cut in thin slices, then fill up your Pie with sharp Apples, and a little Pepper, and a little Salt, then close it, and bake it, then butter it, and serve it in hot to the Table.

93. *To fry Pompion.*

Cut it in thin slices when it is pared, and steep it in Sack a while, then dip it in Eggs, and fry it in Butter, and put some Sack and Butter for Sauce, so serve it in with salt about the Dish brims.

94. *To make Misers for Children to eat in Afternoons in Summer.*

Take half a Pint of good small Beer, two spoonfuls of Sack, the Crum of half a penny Manchet, two handfuls of Currans washed clean and dried, and a little of grated Nutmeg, and a little Sugar, so give it to them cold.

95. *To fry Toasts.*

Take a twopenny white Loaf, and pare away the Crust, and cut thin slices of it, then dip them first in Cream, then in the yolks of Eggs well beaten, and mixed with beaten Cinamon, then fry them in Butter, and serve them in with Verjuice, Butter and Sugar.

96. *To boil or rather stew Carps in their own Blood.*

Take two fair Carps, and scowr them very well from slime with water and a little salt, then lay them in a Dish and open their bellies, take away their Guts, and save the Blood and Rows in the Dish, then put in a Pint of Claret Wine, some whole Spice and some Salt, with a little Horse-Radish Root, then cover them close, and let them stew over a Chafingdish of Coals, and when they are enough, lay them into a Dish which must be rubbed with a Shelots, and Sippets laid in, then take a little of the Liquor, and an Anchovie or two, with a little Butter, heat them together, and pour it over them, then garnish your Dish with Capers, Oranges or Limons, and serve it in very hot.

97. *To make Fritters.*

Take half a Pint of Sack and a Pint of Ale, a little Yest, the yolks of twelve Eggs, and six Whites, with some beaten Spice and a very little salt, make this into thick Batter with fine Flower, then boil your Lard, and dip round thin slices of Apples in this Batter, and fry them; serve them in with beaten spice and sugar.

98. *To pickle Coleflowers.*

Take some white wine Vinegar and salt, with some whole Spice, boil them together very well, then put in your Coleflowers, and cover them, and let them stand upon Embers for one hour, then take them out, and when they are cold, put them into a Pot, and boil the Liquor again with more Vinegar, and when it is cold, put it to them, and keep them close from the Air.

99. *To preserve Orange or Limon Pills in thin slices in Jelly.*

Take the most beautiful and thickest Rinds, and then cut them in halves, and take their Meat clean out, then boil them in several waters till a straw will run through them, then wash them in cold water, and pick them and dry them:

Then take to a Pound of these, one quart of water wherein thin slices of Pippins have been boiled, and that the water feels slippery, take to this water three pounds of Sugar, and make thereof a Syrup, then put in your

Pills and scald them, and set them by till the next day, then boil them till you find that the Syrup will jelly, then lay your Pills into your Glasses, and put into your Syrup the Juice of three Oranges and one Limon; then boil it again till it be a stiff Jelly, and put it to them.

100. *To make Cakes of the Pulp of Limons, or rather the Juice of Limons.*

Take out all the juice part of the Limon without breaking the little skins which hold it, then boil some Sugar to a Candy height, and put in this Juice, and stir it about, and immediately put it into a warm Stove, and put in fire twice or thrice a day; when you see that it doth Candy on the one side, then turn them out of the Glasses with a wet knife on the other upon a sleeked Paper, and then let that candy also, and put them up in a Box with Papers between them.

101. *To make good minced Pies.*

Take one pound and half of Veal parboiled, and as much Suet, shred them very fine, then put in 2 pound of Raisins, 2 pound of Currans, 1 pound of Prunes, 6 Dates, some beaten Spice, a few Caraway seeds, a little Salt, Verjuice, Rosewater and Sugar, to fill your Pies, and let them stand one hour in the Oven:

When they go to Table strew on fine Sugar.

102. *To make a Loaf of Curds.*

Take the Curds of three quarts of Milk rubbed together with a little Flower, then put in a little beaten Ginger, and a little Salt, half a Pint of Yest, the yolks of ten Eggs, and three Whites: work these into a stiff Paste with so much Flower as you see fit, then lay it to rise in a warm Cloth a while, then put in Butter, Sugar, Sack, and some beaten Spice, and so serve it in.

103. *To make Cheese Loaves.*

Take the Curds of three quarts of Milk, and as much grated Bread as Curd, the yolks of twelve Eggs, and six Whites, some Cream, a little Flower, and beaten Spice, a little Salt, and a little Sack; when you have made it in a stiff Paste with a little flower, roul some of it thin to fry, and serve them in with beaten Spice and Sugar strewed over them.

Then make the rest into a Loaf, and bake it, then cut it open, and serve it in with Cream, Butter and Sugar.

104. *To fry Oysters.*

Take of your largest Oysters, wash them and dry them, and beat an Egg or two very well, and dip them in that, and so fry them, then take their Liquor, and put an Anchovy to it, and some Butter, and heat them together over the fire, and having put your fryed Oysters in a Dish, pour the Sawce over them and serve them in.

105. *To broil Oysters.*

Take your largest Oysters, and put them into Scollop Shells, or into the biggest Oyster shells with their own Liquor, and set them upon a Gridiron over Charcoals, and when you see they be boiled in the Liquor, put in some Butter, a few Crums of Bread, and a little Salt, then let them stand till they are very brown, and serve them to the Table in the Shells upon a Dish and Pie-Plate.

106. *To rost Oysters.*

Take the largest, and spit them upon little long sticks, and tie them to the Spit, then lay them down to the fire, and when they are dry, bast them with Claret Wine, and put into your Pan two Anchovies, and two or three Bay-leaves, when you think they are enough, bast them with Butter, and dredge them, and take a little of that liquor in the Pan, and some Butter, and heat it in a Porringer, and pour over them.

107. *To make most excellent and delicate Pies.*

Take two Neats tongues tenderly boiled, and peel them, and mince them small with some Beef Suet or Marrow, then take a pound of Currans and a pound of Raisins of the Sun stoned, some beaten Spice, Rosewater, a little Salt, a little Sack and Sugar.

Beat all these with the minced meat in a Mortar till it come to a perfect Paste, then having your Paste ready laid in your baking-Pan, fill it or them with this meat, then lay on the top some sliced Dates, and so close them, and bake them, when they are cold they will cut smooth like Marmalade.

108. *To make fine Custards.*

Take two quarts of Cream and boil it well with whole Spice, then put in the yolks of twelve Eggs, and six Whites well beaten and strained, then put in these Eggs over the fire, and keep them stirring lest they turn, then when they are thoroughly hot, take it off and stir it till it be almost cold, then put in Rosewater and Sugar, and take out the whole Spice, then put your Custard into several things to bake, and do not let them stand too long in the Oven; when you serve them in, strew on small French Comfits of divers colours, or else fine Sugar, which you please.

109. *To make a Stump Pie.*

Take a pound of Veal and as much Suet, parboil your Veal, and shred them together, but not very small, then put in one pound of Raisins, one pound of Currans, four Ounces of Dates stoned and sliced thin, some beaten Spice, Rosewater and Sugar, and a little Salt, then take the yolks of Eggs well beaten, and mix amongst the rest of the things very well, then having your Pie ready, fill it and press it down, then lid it, and bake it.

110. *To make Egg-Pies.*

Take the yolks of eight hard Eggs, and shred them small with their weight of Beef Suet minced very small also, then put in one pound of Currans, four Ounces of Dates stoned and sliced, some beaten Spice, Limon pill, Rosewater and Sugar, and a little Salt, mix them well together, if you please, you may put in an Apple shred small, so fill your Pies and bake them, but not too much, serve them to the Table with a little Wine.

111. *To make hashed Meat.*

Take a Leg or Shoulder of Mutton, lay it down to the fire, and as it doth rost, cut it off in little bits, and let it lie in the Pan, bast it with Claret wine and Butter, and a little Salt, and put two or three Shelots in your Pan, when you have cut off so much as you can, lay the bones into a Dish over a Chafingdish of Coals, and put your Meat to it with the Liquor, and two

Anchovies, cover it, and let it stew a while; when it is enough, put in some Capers, and serve it in with Sippets; Garnish your Dish with Olives and Capers, and Samphire; thus you may do with any cold meat between two Dishes.

112. *To make a Fricasie of Oysters.*

Take a quart of Oysters and put them into a frying pan with some white Wine and their own Liquor, a little Salt, and some whole Spice, and two or three Bay Leaves, when you think they be enough, lay them in a dish well warmed, then add to their Liquor two Anchovies, some Butter, and the yolks of four Eggs; Garnish your Dish with Barberries.

113. *To make a Fricasie of Eels.*

Take a midling sort of Eels, scour them well, and cut off the heads and throw them away, then gut them, and cut them in pieces, then put them into a frying pan with so much white Wine and water as will cover them, then put in whole Spice, a bundle of sweet herbs and a little Salt, let them boil, and when they be very tender, take them up and lay them into a warm Dish, then add to their Liquor two Anchovies, some Butter and the yolks of Eggs, and pour over them:

Thus you may make Fricasies of Cockles or of Shrimps, or Prawns.

Garnish your Dish with Limon and Barberries.

114. *To make an Eel-Pie.*

Take your largest Eels, and flay them, and cut them in pieces, then having your Pie ready with Butter in the bottom, season your Eels with Pepper, Salt and Nutmeg, then lay them in and cover them with Butter, so close it and bake it, if you please, you may put in some Raisins of the Sun, and some large Mace, it is good hot or cold.

115. *To souce an Eel and Collar it.*

Take a very large fat Eel and scour it well, throw away the head and gut her, and slit her down the back, season her with Pepper, Salt, Nutmeg and Mace, then boil her in white Wine, and Salt and Water, with a bundle of sweet herbs and some Limon Pill, when it is well boiled, take it up and lay it to cool; then put good store of Vinegar into the Liquor, and when it is cold, put in your Eel, and keep it:

You must roul it up in a Collar and tie it hard with a Tape, and sew it up in a Cloth, then put it in to boil; when it hath lain a week, serve it to the Table with a Rosemary Branch in the middle, and Bay Leaves round the Dish sides, eat it with Mustard.

116. *To stew Eels.*

Take them without their heads, flay them and cut them in pieces, then fill a Posnet with them, and set them all on end one by one close to one another, and put in so much White Wine and Water as will cover them, then put in good store of Currans to them, whole Spice, sweet herbs, and a little Salt, cover them and let them stew, and when they are very tender, put in some Butter, and so shake them well, and serve them upon Sippets; Garnish your Dish with Orange or Limon and raw Parsley.

117. *To make a Herring Pie.*

Take four of the best pickled Herrings, and skin them, then split them and bone them, then having your Pie in readiness with Butter in the bottom, then lay your Herrings in halves into your Pie one lay of them, then put in Raisins, Currans and Nutmeg, and a little Sugar, then lay in more Butter, then more Herrings, Fruit and Spice, and more Butter, and so close it, and bake it; your Herrings must be well watered.

118. *To rost a Pike and to lard it.*

Take a large Pike, and scale it, gut it, and wash it clean, then lard it on the back with pickled Herring and Limon Pill, then spit it and lay it down to the fire to rost, bast it often with Claret Wine and Butter, when it is enough, make Sauce for it with Claret Wine and Butter, and serve it in.

119. *To boil fresh Salmon.*

Take a Joll or a Tail of fresh Salmon, then take Vinegar and Water, Salt and whole Spice, and boil them together, then put in your Salmon, and when it is boiled, take some Butter and some of the Liquor with an Anchovie or two, and a little white Wine and a quart of Shrimps out of their Shells, heat these together, and so Dish your Salmon, and pour this over it.

Garnish your Dish with Shrimps and Anchovies, and Slices of Limon.

120. *To boil a Cods Head.*

Boil Wine, Water and Salt together, with whole Spice and sweet herbs, and a little Horse-Radish Root, then put in your Cods head, and boil it very well, then drain it well from the Water, and lay it in a dish over a Chafingdish of Coals:

Then take some of the Liquor and two Anchovies, some butter and some Shrimps, heat them over the fire, and pour over it, then poach some Eggs and lay over it, and also about the Brims of the Dish; Garnish your Dish with Limon and Barberries, so serve it to the Table very hot:

Thus you may do Haddocks or Whitings, or any other fresh Fish you like best.

121. *To make Olives of Veal.*

Take thin slices of a Leg of Veal, and have ready some Suet finely shred, some Currans, beaten Spice, sweet herbs, and hard yolks of Eggs, and a little salt mixed well together, then strew it upon the insides of your slices of Meat, and roul them up hard, and make them fast with a scure, so spit them and roste them, baste them with Butter, and serve them in with Vinegar, Butter and Sugar.

122. *To make an Olive Pie.*

Having your Paste in readiness with Butter in the bottom, lay in some of the forenamed Olives, but not fastned with a Scure, then put in Currans, hard Eggs, and sweet Butter, with some herbs shred fine; be sure you cover it well with Butter, and put in a little white Wine and Sugar, and close it, and bake it, eat it hot or cold, but hot is better.

123. *To make a Ball to take Stains out of Linnen, which many times happens by Cooking or Preserving.*

Take four Ounces of hard white Sope, beat it in a Mortar, with two small Limons sliced, and as much Roch Allom as a Hazle Nut, when they are beaten well together, make it up in little Balls, rub the stain therewith and then wash it in warm water, till you see it be quite out.

124. *To make a fine Pomander.*

Take two Ounces of Laudanum, of Benjamin and Storax one Ounce, Musk six gr. as much of Civet, as much of Ambergreece, of Calamus Aromaticus, and Lignum Aloes, of each the weight of a Groat, beat all these in a hot Mortar and with a hot Pestel, till it come to a perfect Paste, then take a little Gum Dragon steeped in Rosewater, and rub your hand withal, and make it up with speed, and dry them, but first make them into what shapes you please, and print them.

125. *A very fine washing-Ball.*

Take three Ounces of Orrice, half an Ounce of Cypress-wood, 2 Ounces of Calamus Aromaticus, 1 ounce of Damask-Rose leaves, 2 Ounces of Lavender-flowers, a quarter of an Ounce of Cloves, beat all these and searce them fine, then take two pounds and an half of Castile Sope dissolved in Rose water, and beat all these forenamed things with the Sope in a Mortar, and when they are well incorporated, make it into Balls, and keep them in a Box with Cotton as long as you please.

126. *To make French Broth called Kink.*

Take a leg of Beef and set it over the fire with a good quantity of fair water, when it boils, scum it, and what meat soever you have to dress that day, either of Fowl or small meat, put it all into this Liquor and parboil it, then take out those small meats, and put in some French Barley, and some whole Spice, one Clove or two of Garlick, and a handful of Leeks, and some Salt; when it is boiled enough, pour it from the Barley, and in put a little Saffron; so serve it in; and garnish your Dish with sliced Oranges or Limons, and put a little of the juice therein.

127. *To make Broth of a Lambs Head.*

Boil it with as much water as will cover it, with whole Spice, and a little Salt, and a bundle of sweet herbs, then put in strained Oatmeal and Cream, and some Currans, when you take it up, put in Sack and Sugar, then lay the Head in a Dish, and put the Broth to it, and serve it in.

128. *To season a Chicken-Pie.*

Having your Paste rolled thin, and laid into your baking-pan, lay in some Butter, then lay in your Chickens quartered, and seasoned with Pepper, Nutmeg and a little Salt, then put in Raisins, Currans, and Dates, then lay Butter on the top, close it and bake it, then cut it up, and put in Clouted Cream, Sack and Sugar.

129. *To make an Herb Pie.*

Take Spinage, hard Lettice, and a few sweet herbs, pick them, wash them, and shred them, and put them into your Pie with Butter, and Nutmeg and Sugar, and a little Salt, to close it and bake it, then draw it and open it, and put in Clouted Cream; Sack and Sugar, and stir it well together, and serve it in.

130. *To roste Lobsters.*

Take two fair Lobsters alive, wash them clean, and stop the holes as you do to boil, then fasten them to a Spit, the insides together; make a good fire, and strew Salt on them, and that will kill them quickly, bast them with Water and Salt till they be very red, then have ready some Oysters stewed and cut small; put them into a Dish with melted Butter beaten thick with a little water, then take a few spoonfuls of the Liquor of the stewed Oysters, and dissolve in it two Anchovies, then put it to the melted Butter, then take up your Lobsters, and crack the shells that they may be easie to open.

131. *To make a Pumpion Pie.*

Take a Pumpion, pare it, and cut it in thin slices, dip it in beaten Eggs and Herbs shred small, and fry it till it be enough, then lay it into a Pie with Butter, Raisins, Currans, Sugar and Sack, and in the bottom some sharp Apples; when it is baked, butter it and serve it in.

132. *To make an Artichoke Pudding.*

Boil a quart of Cream with whole Spice, then put in half a pound of sweet Almonds blanched, and beaten with Rosewater; when they have boiled well, take it from the fire, and take out the Spice, when it is almost cold, put in the yolks of ten Eggs, some Marrow and some bottoms of Artichokes, then sweeten it with Sugar and put in a little Salt, then butter a Dish, and bake it in it, serve it to the Table stuck full of blanched Almonds, and fine Sugar strewed over it.

133. *To pickle Sprats like Anchovies.*

Take a Peck of the biggest Sprats without their heads, and salt them a little over night, then take a Pot or Barrel, and lay in it a Lay of Bay salt, and then a lay of Sprats, and a few Bay leaves, then salt again; thus do till you have filled the Vessel, put in a little Limon Pill also among your Bay leaves, then cover the Vessel and pitch it, that no Air get in, set it in a cool Cellar, and once in a week turn it upside down; in three Months you may eat of them.

134. *To keep Artichokes all the Year.*

Gather your Artichokes with long stalks, and then cut off the stalks close to them, then boil some water, with good Pears and Apples sliced thin, and the Pith of the great stalks, and a Quince or two quartered to give it a relish; when these have boiled a while, put in your Artichokes, and boil all together till they be tender, then take them up and set them to cool, then boil your Liquor well and strain it, when your Artichokes be cold, put them into your Barrel, and when the Liquor is cold, pour it over them, so cover it close that no Air get in.

135. *To make Pasty of a Joll of Ling.*

Make your Crust with fine Flower, Butter, cold Cream, and two yolks of Eggs:

Roul it thin and lay it in your Bake-pan, then take part of a Joll of Ling well boiled, and pull it all in Bits, then lay some Butter into your Pasty and then the Ling, then some grated Nutmeg, sliced Ginger, Cloves and Mace, Oysters, Muscles, Cockles, and Shrimps, the yolks of raw Eggs, a few Comfits perfumed, Candied Orange Pill, Citron Pill, and Limon Pill, with Eringo Roots:

Then put in white Wine, and good store of Butter, and put on a thick lid, when it is baked, open it, and let out the steam.

136. *To make French Servels.*

Take cold Gammon of Bacon, fat and lean together, cut it small as for Sausages, season it with Pepper, Cloves and Mace, and a little Shelots, knead it into a Paste with the yolks of Eggs, and fill some Bullocks Guts with it, and boil them; but if you would have them to keep, then do not put in Eggs.

When you have filled the Guts, boil them, and hang them up, and when you would eat them, serve them in thin slices with a Sallad.

137. *To make a Pallat Pie.*

Take Oxe Pallats and boil them so tender that you may run a straw through them; to three Palates take six Sheeps tongues boiled tender and peeled, three sweet-Breads of Veal, cut all these in thin slices, then having your Pie ready, and Butter in the bottom, lay in these things, first seasoned with Pepper, Salt and Nutmeg, and Thyme and Parsley shred small, and as the Season of the year is, put into it Asparagus, Anchovies, Chesnuts, or what you please else, as Candied Orange Pill, Limon Pill, or Citron Pill, with Eringo roots, and yolks of hard Eggs, some Marrow and some Oysters, then lay in good store of Butter on the top, so close it and bake it, then put in white Wine, buter, the yolks of Eggs, and Vinegar and Sugar; heat them together over the fire, and serve it in.

138. *To make Sauce for Fowles or Mutton.*

Take Claret Wine, Vinegar, Anchovies, Oisters, Nutmeg, Shelot, Gravie of Mutton or Beef, sweet Butter, Juice of Limon, and a little Salt, and if you please Orange or Limon Pill.

139. *To make Oat-Cakes.*

Take fine Flower, and mix it very well with new Ale Yest, and make it very stiff, then make it into little Cakes, and roul them very thin, then lay them on an Iron to bake, or on a baking stone, and make but a slow fire under it, and as they are baking, take them and turn the edges of them round on the Iron, that they may bake also, one quarter of an hour will bake them; a little before you take them up, turn them on the other side, only to flat them; for if you turn them too soon, it will hinder the rising, the Iron or Stone whereon they are baked, must stand at a distance from the fire.

140. *To make a rare Lamb Pie.*

Take a Leg of Lamb, and take the meat clean out of it at the great end, but keep the skin whole, then press the Meat in a Cloth, and mince it small, and put as much Beef Suet to it as the Meat in weight, and mince it small, then put to it Naples Bisket grated fine, season it with beaten Spice, Rosewater, and a little Salt, then put in some Candied Limon Pill, Orange Pill, and Citron Pill shred small, and some Sugar, then put part of the Meat into the skin, then having your Pie in readiness, and Butter in the bottom, lay in this Meat, then take the rest of your Meat, and make it into Balls or Puddings with yolks of Eggs, then lay them into the Pie to fill up the Corners, then take Candied Orange, Limon and Citron Pill, cut in long narrow slices and strew over it; you may put in Currans and Dates if you please, then lay on Butter, and close up your Pie and bake it, and leave a Tunnel, when it is baked, put in Sack, Sugar, yolks of Eggs and Butter heat together, if you put in Marrow, it will be the better.

141. *To fry Garden Beans.*

Boil them and blanch them, and fry them in Sweet Butter, with Parsley and shred Onions and a little Salt, then melt Butter for the Sauce.

142. *To make a Sorrel Sallad.*

Take a quantity of French Sorrel picked clean and washed, boil it with water and a little Salt, and when it is enough, drain it and butter it, and put in a little Vinegar and Sugar into it, then garnish it with hard Eggs and Raisins.

143. *To make good cold Sallads of several things.*

Take either Coleflowers, or Carrots, or Parsneps, or Turneps after they are well boiled, and serve them in with Oil, Vinegar and Pepper, also the Roots of red Beets boiled tender are very good in the same manner.

144. *To make the best sort of Pippin Paste.*

Take a pound of raw Pippins sliced and beaten in a Mortar, then take a pound of fine Sugar and boil it to a candy height with a little fair water, then put in your Pippins, and boil it till it will come from the bottom of the Posnet, but stir it for fear it burn.

145. *To make Sauce for a Leg of Veal rosted.*

Take boiled Currans, and boiled Parsley, and hard Eggs and Butter and Sugar hot together.

146. *To make Sauce for a Leg of Mutton rosted with Chesnuts.*

Take a good quantity of Chesnuts, and boil them tender, then take the shells off, and bruise them small, then put to them Claret Wine, Butter and a little Salt, so put it into the Dish to the Meat, and serve it in.

147. *To keep Quinces white, either to preserve whole, or for white Marmalade or Paste.*

Coddle them with white Wine and Water, and cover them with sliced Pippins in the Codling.

148. *To make little Pasties with sweet Meats to fry.*

Make some Paste with cold water, butter and flower, with the yolk of an Egg, then roul it out in little thin Cakes, and lay one spoonful of any kind of Sweet meats you like best upon every one, so close them up and fry them with Butter, and serve them in with fine Sugar strewed on.

149. *To boil a Capon on the French fashion.*

Boil your Capon in water and salt, and a little dusty Oatmeal to make it look white, then take two or three Ladles full of Mutton Broth, a Faggot of sweet herbs, two or three Dates cut in long pieces, a few parboiled Currans, and a little whole Pepper, a little Mace and Nutmeg, thicken it with Almonds; season it with Verjuice, Sugar, and a little sweet Butter, then take up your Capon and lard it well with preserved Limon, then lay it in a deep Dish, and pour the broth upon it; then Garnish your Dish with Suckets and preserved Barberries.

150. *To Souce a Pike, Carp or Bream.*

Draw your Fish, but scale it not, and save the Liver of it; wash it very well, then take white Wine, as much water again as Wine, boil them together with whole Spice, Salt and a bundle of sweet Herbs, and when boiles put in your Fish, and just before it a little Vinegar; for that will make it crisp: when it is enough, take it up and put it into a Trey, then put into the Liquor some whole Pepper, and whole Ginger, and when it is boiled enough, take it off and cool it, and when it is quite cold, put in your Fish, and when you serve it in, lay some of the Jelly about the Dish sides, and some Fennel and Sawcers of Vinegar.

151. *To boil a Gurnet on the French fashion.*

Draw your Gurnet and wash it, boil it in water and salt and a bundle of sweet herbs; when it is enough, take it up and put it into a Dish with Sippets over a Chafingdish of Coals; then take Verjuice, Butter, Nutmeg and Pepper, and the yolks of two Eggs, heat it together, and pour over it; Garnish your Dish as you please.

152. *To rost a Leg of Mutton on the French fashion.*

Take a Leg of Mutton, and pare off all the Skin as thin as you can, then lard it with sweet Lard, and stick it with Cloves, when it is half rosted, cut off three or four thin pieces, and mince it with sweet herbs, and a little beaten Ginger, put in a Ladle full of Claret wine, and a little sweet butter, two sponfuls of Verjuice and a little Pepper, a few Capers, then chop the yolks of two hard Eggs in it, then when these have stewed a while in a Dish, put your bonie part which is rosted into a Dish, and pour this on it and serve it in.

153. *To rost a Neats tongue.*

Chop sweet herbs fine with a piece of raw Apple, season it with Pepper and Ginger, and the yolk of an Egg made hard and minced small, then stuff your Tongue with this, and rost it well, and baste it with Butter and Wine; when it is enough, take Verjuice, Butter, and the Juice of a Limon, and a little Nutmeg, then Dish your Tongue and pour this Sauce over it and serve it in.

154. *To boil Pigeons with Rice.*

Take your Pigeons and truss them, and stuff their bellies with sweet herbs, then put them into a Pipkin with as much Mutton broth as will cover them, with a blade of Mace and some whole Pepper; boil all these together until the Pigeons be tender, and put in Salt:

Then take them from the fire, and scum off the Fat very clean, then put in a piece of sweet Butter, season it with Verjuice, Nutmeg and a little Sugar, thicken it with Rice boiled in sweet Cream. Garnish your Dish with preserved Barberries and Skirret Roots boiled tender.

155. *To boil a Rabbit.*

Take a large Rabbit, truss it and boil it with a little Mutton Broth, white Wine and a blade of Mace, then take Lettuce, Spinage, and Parsley, Winter-Savory and sweet Marjoram, pick all these and wash them clean, and bruise them a little to make the Broth look green, thicken it with the Crust of a Manchet first steeped in a little Broth, and put in a little sweet Butter, season it with Verjuice and Pepper, and serve it to the Table upon Sippets; Garnish the Dish with Barberries.

156. *To boil a Teal or Wigeon.*

Parboil either of these Fowls and throw them into a pail of fair Water, for that taketh away the Rankness, then rost them half, and take them from the fire, and put sweet herbs in the bellies of them, and stick the Brests with Cloaves, then put them in a Pipkin with two or three ladles full of Mutton broth, very strong of the Meat, a blade of whole Mace, two or three little Onions minced small; thicken it with a Toast of Houshold bread, and put in a little Butter, then put in a little Verjuice, so take it up and serve it.

157. *To boil Chickens or Pigeons with Goosberries or Grapes.*

Boil them with Mutton Broth and white Wine, with a blade of Mace and a little Salt, and let their bellies be filled with sweet herbs, when they are tender thicken the Broth with a piece of Manchet, and the yolks of two hard Eggs, strained with some of the Broth, and put it into a deep Dish with some Verjuice and Butter and Sugar, then having Goosberries or Grapes tenderly scalded, put them into it, then lay your Chickens or Pigeons into a Dish, and pour the Sauce over them, and serve them in.

158. *A made Dish of Rabbits Livers.*

Take six Livers and chop them fine with sweet herbs and the yolks of two hard Eggs, season it with beaten Spice, and Salt, and put in some plumped Currans, and a little melted Butter, so mix them very well together, and having some Paste ready rouled thin, make it into little Pasties and fry them, strew Sugar over them and serve them.

159. *To make a Florentine with the Brawn of a Capon, or the Kidney of Veal.*

Mince any of these with sweet Herbs, then put in parboiled Currans, and Dates minced small, and a little Orange or Limon Pill which is Candied shred small, season it with beaten Spice and Sugar, then take the yolks of two hard Eggs and bruise them with a little Cream, a piece of a short Cake grated, and Marrow cut in short pieces, mix all these together with the forenamed Meat, and put in a little Salt and a little Rosewater, and bake it in a Dish in a Puff-Past, and when you serve it strew Sugar over it.

160. *A Friday Pie without Fish or Flesh.*

Wash a good quantity of green Beets, and pluck out the middle string, then chop them small, with two or three ripe Apples well relished, season it with Pepper, Salt, and Ginger, then add to it some Currans, and having your Pie ready, and Butter in the bottom, put in these herbs, and with them a little Sugar, then put Butter on the top, and close and bake it, then cut it up, and put in the juice of a Limon and Sugar.

161. *To make Umble Pies.*

Boil them very tender, and mince them very small with Beef Suet and Marrow then season it with beaten Spice and Salt, Rosewater and Sugar and a little Sack, so put it into your Paste with Currans and Dates.

162. *To bake Chickens with Grapes.*

Scald your Chickens and truss them, and season them with Pepper, Salt and Nutmeg, and having your Pie ready, and Butter laid in the bottom, put in your Chickens, and then more butter, and bake them with a thin Lid on

You may bake it if you please in a baking-pan.

176. *To make a Pudding of Goose Blood.*

Save the blood of a Goose, and strain it, then put in fine Oatmeal steeped in warm Milk, Nutmeg, Pepper, sweet Herbs, Sugar, Salt, Suet minced fine, Rosewater, Limon Pill, Coriander seeds, then put in some Eggs, and beat all these together very well, then boil them how you do like, either in a buttered Cloth or in Skins, or rost it within the Neck of the Goose.

177. *To make Liver Puddings.*

Take a Hogs Liver boiled and cold, grate it like Bread, then take new Milk and the Fat of a Hog minced fine, put it to the Bread and the Liver, and divide it into two parts, then dry herbs or other if you can minced fine, and put the Herbs into one part with beaten Spice, Anniseeds, Rosewater, Cream and Eggs, Sugar and Salt, so fill the Skins and boil them.

To the other part put preserved Barberries, diced Dates, Currans, beaten Spice, Salt, Sugar, Rosewater, Cream and Eggs, so mix them well together, and fill the Skins and boil them.

178. *To make a Chiveridge Pudding.*

Take the fattest Guts of your Hog clean scoured, then fluff them with beaten Spice and sliced Dates, sweet herbs, a little Salt, Rosewater, Sugar, and two or three Eggs to make it slide; so fill them, tie them up like Puddings and boil them; when they are enough serve them.

179. *To make Rice Puddings in Skins.*

Take two quarts of Milk and put therein as it is yet cold, two good handfuls of Rice clean picked and washed, set it over a slow fire and stir it often, but gently; when you perceive it to swell, let it boil apace till it be tender and very thick, then take it from the fire, and when it is cold, put in six Eggs well beaten, some Rosewater and Sugar, beaten Spice and a little Salt, preserved Barberries and Dates minced small, some Marrow and Citron Pill; mingle them well together and fill your Skins, and boil them.

180. *To make a stewed Pudding.*

Take the yolks of three Eggs and one White, six spoonfuls of sweet Cream, a little beaten spice, and a quarter of a pound of Sewet minced fine, a quarter of a pound of Currans, and a little grated bread, Rosewater, Sugar and Salt; mingle them well together, and wrap them up in little pieces of the Cawl of Veal, and fasten them with a little stick, and tie each end with a stick, you may put four in one dish, then take half a pint of strong Mutton Broth, and 6 spoonfuls of Vinegar, three or four blades of large Mace, and one Ounce of Sugar, make this to boil over a Chafingdish of Coals, then put in your Puddings, and when they boil, cover them with another Dish, but turn them sometimes, and when you see that they are enough, take your Puddings and lay them in a warm Dish upon Sippets, then add to their Broth some Sack, Sugar, and Butter, and pour over them; garnish your Dish with Limon and Barberries.

181. *To make a* Sussex *Pudding.*

Take a little cold Cream, Butter and Flower, with some beaten Spice, Eggs, and a little Salt, make them into a stiff Paste, then make it up in a round Ball, and as you mold it, put in a great piece of Butter in the middle; and so tye it hard up in a buttered Cloth, and put it into boiling water, and let it boil apace till it be enough, then serve it in, and garnish your dish with Barberries; when it is at the Table cut it open at the top, and there will be as it were a Pound of Butter, then put Rosewater and Sugar into it, and so eat it.

In some of this like Paste you may wrap great Apples, being pared whole, in one piece of thin Paste, and so close it round the Apple, and throw them into boiling water, and let them boil till they are enough, you may also put some green Goosberries into some, and when either of these are boiled, cut them open and put in Rosewater Butter and Sugar.

182. *To make* French *Puffs.*

Take Spinage Parsley and Endive, with a little Winter savory, and wash them, and mince them very fine; season them with Nutmeg, Ginger and Sugar, season them with Eggs, and put in a little Salt, then cut a Limon into thin round slices, and upon every slice of Limon lay one spoonful of it.

Then fry them, and serve them in upon some Sippets, and pour over them Sack, Sugar and butter.

183. *To make Apple Puffs.*

Take a Pomewater, or any other Apple that is not hard or harsh in taste, mince it with a few Raisins of the Sun stoned, then wet them with Eggs, and beat them together with the back of a Spoon, season them with Nutmeg, Rosewater, Sugar, and Ginger, drop them into a frying pan with a Spoon into hot Butter, and fry them, then serve them in with the juice of an Orange and a little Sugar and Butter.

184. *To make Kickshaws, to bake or fry in what shape you please.*

Take some Puff-paste and roul it thin, if you have Moulds work it upon them with preserved Pippins, and so close them, and fry or bake them, but when you have closed them you must dip them in the yolks of Eggs, and that will keep all in; fill some with Goosberries, Rasberries, Curd, Marrow, Sweet-breads, Lambs Stones, Kidney of Veal, or any other thing what you like best, either of them being seasoned before you put them in according to your mind, and when they are baked or fryed, strew Sugar on them, and serve them in.

185. *To make an* Italian *Pudding.*

Take a penny white loaf and pare off the crust, then cut it like Dice, then take some Beef Suet shred small, and half a pound of Raisins of the Sun stoned, with as many Currans, mingle them together and season them with beaten Spice and a little Salt, wet them with four Eggs, and stir them gently for fear of breaking the Bread, then put it in a dish with a little Cream and Rosewater and Sugar, then put in some Marrow and Dates, and so butter a dish and bake it, then strew on Sugar and serve it.

186. *To hash Calves Tongues.*

Boil them tender and pill them, then lard them with Limon Pill, and lard them also with fat Bacon, then lay them to the Fire and half rost them; then put them in a Pipkin with Claret Wine, whole Spice and sliced Limon, and a few Caraway Seeds, a little Rosemary and a little Salt, boil all together and serve them in upon Toasts. Thus you may do with Sheeps Tongues also.

187. *To boil a Capon.*

Take strong Mutton Broth, and truss a Capon, and boil him in it with some Marrow and a little Salt in a Pipkin, when it is tender, then put in a pint of White Wine, half a pound of Sugar, and four Ounces of Dates stoned and sliced, Potato Roots boiled and blanched, large Mace and Nutmeg sliced, boil all these together with a quarter of a pint of Verjuyce, then dish the Capon, and add to the Broth the yolks of six Eggs beaten with Sack, and so serve it; garnish dish with several sorts of Candied Pills and Preserved Barberries, and sliced Limon with Sugar upon every slice.

188. *To boil a Capon with Rice.*

Truss your Capon and boil him in water and salt, then take a quarter of a pound of Rice, first boiled in Milk, and put in with some whole Spice and a little Salt, when it is almost enough put in a little Rosewater, and half a pound of Almonds blanched and beaten, strain them in, and put in some Cream and Sugar, then when your Capon is enough, lay it in a dish, and pour the Broth thereon; garnish your Dish as you please, and serve it in.

189. *To boil a Capon with Pippins.*

Parboil your capon after it is trussed, then put it into a pipkin with Mutton Broth and Marrow, and a little Salt, with a quart of White-Wine, a little Nutmeg and Dates stoned and sliced, then put in a quarter of a pound of fine Sugar, then take some Pippins stewed with Sugar, Spice and a little water, and put them in, then lay your Capon into a Dish, and lay some Naples Biskets for Sippets, then bruise the yolks of eight hard Eggs and put into your Broth, with a little Sack, and pour it over your Capon; Garnish your Dish and serve it in.

190. *To boil Chickens with Lettuce the very best way.*

Parboil your Chickens and cut them in Quarters, and put them into a Pipkin with some Mutton Broth, and two or three sweet Breads of Veal, and some Marrow, and some Cloves, and a little Salt, and a little Limon Pill; then take good store of hard Lettuce, cut them in halves and wash them, and put them in; then put in Butter and Sack and white Wine, with a little Mace and Nutmeg, and sliced Dates, let all these stew upon the Fire, and when they be enough, serve them in with Toasts of white Bread for Sippets; Garnish the Dish with Limon and Barberies, and what else you please; thus you may do Pigeons.

190. [Transcriber's Note: so numbered in original] *To boil a Rabbit with Grapes or with Goosberries.*

Truss your Rabbit whole, and boil it in some Mutton Broth till it be tender;

Then take a pint of White Wine, and a good handful of Spinage chopped, the yolks of hard Eggs cut in quarters, put these to the Rabbit with some large Mace; a Fagot of sweet Herbs and a little Salt and some Butter, let them boil together a while, then take your Rabbet and lay it in a Dish and some Sippets, then lay over it some Grapes or Goosberries, scalded with Sugar, and pour your Broth over it.

191. *To boil a Rabbit with Claret Wine.*

Boil a Rabbet as before, then slice Onions and a Carrot root, a few Currans and a Fagot of sweet herbs, and a little Salt, minced Parsley, Barberries picked, large Mace, Nutmeg and Ginger, put all these into a Pipkin with the Rabbet, half a Pound of Butter, and a Pint of Claret

Wine, and let them boil together till it be enough, then serve it upon Sippets.

192. *To boil a wild Duck.*

Truss and parboil it, then half rost it, then carve it, and save the Gravie, then take Onions and Parsley sliced, Ginger and Pepper, put the Gravie into a Pipkin, with Currans, Mace, Barberries, and a quart of Claret Wine, and a little Salt, put your Duck with all the forenamed things into it, and let them boil till it be enough, then put in butter and sugar, and serve it in upon Sippets.

193. *To boil a tame Duck.*

Take your Duck and truss it, and boil it with water and salt, or rather Mutton broth, when it hath boiled a while, put in some whole Spice, and when it is boiled enough, take some white wine and butter, and good store of Onions boiled tender in several waters, with a little of the Liquor wherein the Duck hath boiled, and a little Salt: put your Duck into a Dish, and heat these things together and pour over it; and serve it; garnish the Dish with boiled Onions and Barberries.

194. *To boil Pigeons with Capers and Samphire.*

Truss your Pigeons, and put them into a Pipkin with some Mutton broth and white Wine, a bundle of sweet herbs, when they are boiled, lay them into a Dish, then take some of the broth with some Capers and Limon sliced, and some butter, heat these together and pour over them; then fry thin slices of Bacon, and lay upon them, and some Samphire washed from the Salt, and some slices of Limon; Garnish your Dish with the same and serve it in.

195. *To boil Sausages.*

Take two pounds of Sausages, and boil them with a quart of Claret Wine and a bundle of sweet herbs, and whole Cloves and Mace; then put in a little Butter, when they are enough, serve them in with this Liquor and some Mustard in Sawcers.

196. *To boil Goose Giblets.*

Boil them with water and salt, and a bundle of sweet herbs, Onions and whole spice, when they are enough, put in Verjuice and Butter, and some Currans plumped, and serve them upon Sippets.

Thus you may dress Swans Giblets.

197. *To boil Giblets with Roots and good Herbs.*

Boil them in a quart of Claret, Ginger and Cloves, and a Faggot of sweet herbs, Turneps and Carots sliced, with good store of Spinage and a little salt; when they are enough, serve them upon Sippets.

And add to the Broth some Verjuice and the yolks of Eggs; Garnish your Dish with Parsley and pickled Barberries.

198. *To smoor a Neck of Mutton.*

Cut your Steaks, and put them into a Dish with some Butter, then take a Faggot of sweet herbs and some gross Pepper and a little Salt, and put them to them; cover your Dish, and let them stew till they are enough, turning them sometimes, then put in a little Claret Wine and Anchovies, and serve them upon Sippets.

199. *To smoor Veal.*

Cut thin slices of Veal and hack them over with the back of a Knife, then lard them with Lard, and Fry them with strong Beer or Ale till they be enough, then stew them in Claret wine with some whole Spice and Butter and a little salt.

Garnish your Dish with Sausages fryed; and with Barberries, to serve them in.

200. *To smoor Steaks of Mutton another way.*

Cut part of a Leg of Mutton into steaks, and fry it in White Wine and a little salt, a bundle of herbs, and a little Limon Pill, then put it into a Pipkin with some sliced Limon, without the Rind, and some of the Liquor it was fried in, and Butter and a little Parslie, boil all together till you see it be enough, then serve it in, and garnish your Dish with Limon and Barberries.

201. *To smoor Chickens.*

Cut them in Joints and fry them with sweet Butter, then take white Wine, Parsley and Onions chopp'd small, whole Mace and a little gross Pepper, a little Sugar, Verjuice and Butter, let these and your fried Chicken boil together, then fry the Leaves of Clary with Eggs, put in a little Salt to your

Chickens, and when they are enough, serve them in this fried Clary, and garnish your Dish with Barberries.

202. *To fry Museles, or Oysters, or Cockles to serve in with Meat, or by themselves.*

Take any of these and parboil them in their own Liquor, then dry them, flower them, and fry them, then put them into a Pipkin with Claret wine, whole Spice and Anchovies, and a little butter, so let them stew together, and serve them in either with a Duck, or by themselves, as you like best.

204. [Transcriber's note: so numbered in original] *To dress Calves feet.*

Take Calves feet tenderly boiled, and slit them in the middle, then put them in a Dish with sweet Butter, Parsley and Onions chopped a little Thyme, large Mace, Pepper with a little Wine Vinegar, and a little salt, let all these stew together till they are enough, then lay your Calves feet in a Dish, and pour the Sauce over them, then strew some raw Parsley and hard Eggs chopped together over them with slices of Limon and Barberries.

205. *To hash Neats tongues.*

Boil them and blanch them, and slice them thin then take Raisins of the Sun, large Mace, Dates sliced thin, a few blanched Almonds and Claret wine with a little salt; boil all these together with some sweet butter, verjuice and sugar; when they are enough, serve them in and thicken the Sauce with yolks of Eggs; garnish your Dish with Barberries.

206. *Another way to hash Neats Tongues.*

Boil Neats Tongues very tender, peel them and slice them thin, then take strong meat broth, blanched Chesnuts, a Faggot of sweet herbs, large Mace, and Endive, a little Pepper and whole Cloves and a little Salt; boil all these together with some butter till they be enough; garnish your Dish as before.

207. *To boil Chickens in white-broth.*

Take three Chickens and truss them, then take two or three blades of Mace, as many quartered Dates, four or five Lumps of Marrow, a little Salt and a little Sugar, the yolks of three hard Eggs, and a quarter of a Pint of Sack, first boil your Chickins in Mutton broth, and then add these things to them, and let them boil till they are enough, then lay your Chickens in a Dish, and strain some Almonds blanched and beaten into it, serve it upon Sippets of French Bread; garnish your Dish with hard Eggs and Limons.

208. *To boil Partridges.*

Put two or three Partridges into a Pipkin with as much water as will cover them, then put in three or four blades of Mace, one Nutmeg quartered, five or six Cloves, a piece of sweet Butter, two or three Toasts of Manchet toasted brown, soke them in Sack or Muskadine, and break them, and put them into the Pipkin with the rest, and a little Salt, when they are enough, lay them in a Dish, and pour this Broth over them, then garnish your Dish with hard Eggs and sliced Limon, and serve it in.

209. *To boil a Leg of Mutton.*

Take a large Leg of Mutton and stuff it well with Mutton Suet, Salt and Nutmeg, boil it in water and Salt, but not too much, then put some of that broth into another Pot, with three or four blades of Mace, some Currans and

Salt, boil them till half be consumed, then put in some sweet Butter, and some Capers and a Limon cut like Dice with the Rind on, a little Sack, and the yolks of two hard Eggs minced; then lay your Mutton into a Dish upon Sippets, and pour this Sauce over it; scrape Sugar on the sides of your Dish, and lay on slices of Limon and Barberries.

210. *To stew Trouts.*

Put two Trouts into a fair dish with some white Wine, sweet butter, and a little whole Mace, a little Parsley, Thyme and Savory minced, then put in an Anchovy and the yolks of hard Eggs; when your Fish is enough, serve it on Sippets, and pour this over it, and garnish your Dish with Limon and Barberries, and serve them in: you may add Capers to it if you please, and you may do other Fish in this manner.

211. *To boil Eels in Broth to serve with them.*

Flay and wash your Eels and cut them in pieces about a handful long, then put them into a pot with so much Water as will cover them, a little Pepper and Mace, sliced Onions, a little grated bread, and a little Yest, a good piece of sweet butter, some Parsley, Winter Savory and Thyme shred small; let them boil softly half an hour, and put in some Salt, with some Currans; when it is enough, put in Verjuice and more Butter, and so serve it; Garnish your Dish with Parsley, Limon and Barberries, put Sippets in your Dish.

212. *To boil a Pike with Oysters.*

Take a fair Pike and gut it and wash it, and truss it round with the tail in the mouth, then take white Wine, Water and Salt, with a bundle of sweet herbs, and whole Spice, a little Horse-radish; when it boils, tie up your Pike in a Cloth, and put it in, and let it boil till it swims, for then it is enough; then take the Rivet of the Pike, and a Pint of great Oysters with their Liquor, and some Vinegar, large Mace, gross Pepper, then lay your Pike in a Dish with Sippets, and then heat these just named things with some Butter and Anchovies, and pour over it; garnish your Dish as you please.

213. *To make a grand Sallad.*

Take a fair broad brimm'd dish, and in the middle of it lay some pickled Limon Pill, then lay round about it each sort by themselves, Olives, Capers, Broom Buds, Ash Keys, Purslane pickled, and French Beans pickled, and little Cucumbers pickled, and Barberries pickled, and Clove Gilliflowers, Cowslips, Currans, Figs, blanched Almonds and Raisins, Slices of Limon with Sugar on them, Dates stoned and sliced.

Garnish your Dish brims with Candied Orange, Limon and Citron Pill, and some Candied Eringo roots.

214. *To rost Pig with a Pudding in his Belly.*

Take a fat Pig and truss his head backward loking over his back, then make such Pudding as you like best, and fill his belly with it, your Pudding must be stiff, then sew it up, and rost your Pig, when it is almost enough, wring upon it the Juice of a Limon, and when you are ready to take it up, wash it over with yolks of Eggs, and before they can dry, dredge it with grated bread mixed with a little Nutmeg and Ginger, let your Sauce be Vinegar, Butter and Sugar, and the yolks of hard Eggs minced.

215. *To rost a Leg of Mutton with Oisters.*

Take a large Leg of Mutton and stuff it well with Mutton Sewet, with Pepper, Nutmeg Salt and Mace, then rost it and stick it with Cloves, when it is half rosted cut off some of the under side of the fleshy end, in little thin Bits, then take a Pint of Oisters and the Liquor of them, a little Mace, sweet Butter and Salt, put all these with the Bits of Mutton into a Pipkin till half be consumed; then Dish your Mutton and pour this Sauce over it, strew Salt about the Dish side and serve it in.

216. *To make a Steak-Pie.*

Cut a Neck of Mutton in steaks, then season it with Pepper and Salt, lay your Paste into your Baking Pan, and lay Butter in the bottom, then lay in your steaks, and a little large Mace, and cover it with Butter, so close it, and bake it; and against it is baked, have in readiness good store of boiled Parslie minced fine, and drained from the water, some white Wine and some Vinegar, sweet Butter and Sugar, cut open your Pie, and put in this Sauce, and shake it well, and serve it to the Table; it is not so good cold as hot.

217. *To rost a Haunch or a Shoulder of Venison, or a Chine of Mutton.*

Take either of these, and lard it with Lard, and stick it thick with Rosemary, then roft it with a quick fire, but do not lay it too near; baste it with sweet butter: then take half a Pint of Claret wine, a little beaten Cinamon and Ginger, and as much sugar as will sweeten it, five or six whole Cloves, a little grated bread, and when it is boiled enough, put in a little Sweet butter, a little Vinegar, and a very little Salt, when your meat is rosted, serve it in with Sauce, and strew salt about your Dish.

218. *To rost a Capon with Oysters and Chesnuts.*

Take some boiled Chesnuts, and take off their shells, and take as many parboil'd Oysters, then spit your Capon, and put these into the belly of it, with some sweet Butter, rost it and bast it with sweet Butter, save the Gravie, and some of the Chesnuts, and some of the Oysters, then add to them half a Pint of Claret Wine, and a pice of sweet Butter and a little Pepper, and a little Salt, stew these altogether till the Capon be ready, then serve them in with it; Garnish your Dish as you please.

219. *To rost Shoulder or Fillet of Veal with farcing herbs.*

Wash your meat and parboil it a little, then take Parsley, Winter-savory, and Thyme, of each a little minced small, put to them the yolks of three or four hard eggs minced, Nutmeg, Pepper and Currans and Salt, add also some Suet minced small; work all these with the yolk of a raw Egg, and stuff your Meat with it, but save some, and set it under the meat while it doth rost, when your meat is almost rosted enough, put to these in the Dish, a quarter of a pint of White Wine Vinegar, and some Sugar, when your meat is ready, serve it in with this Sauce, and strew on Salt.

220. *To make boiled Sallads.*

Boil some Carots very tender, and scrape them to pieces like the Pulp of an Apple, season them with Cinamon and Ginger and Sugar, put in Currans, a little Vinegar, and a piece of sweet Butter, stew these in a Dish, and when they begin to dry put in more Butter and a little Salt, so serve them to the Table, thus you may do Lettuce, or Spinage or Beets.

221. *To boil a Shoulder of Veal.*

Take a Shoulder of Veal and half boil it in Water and Salt, then slice off the most part of it, and save the Gravie; then take that sliced meat, and put it in a Pot with some of the Broth that boiled it, a little grated Bread, Oister Liquor, Vinegar, Bacon scalded and sliced thin, a Pound of Sausages out of their skins, and rolled in the yolks of Eggs, large Mace and Nutmeg, let these stew about one hour, than put in one Pint of Oisters, some sweet herbs, and a little Salt, stew them together, then take the bone of Veal and broil it and Dish it, then add to your Liquor a little Butter, and some minced Limon with the Rind, a Shelot or two sliced, and pour it over, then lay on it some fryed Oysters; Garnish your Dish with Barberries and sliced Limon, and serve it in.

222. *To boil a Neck of Mutton.*

Boil it in water and salt, then make sauce for it with Samphire and a little of the Broth, Verjuice, large Mace, Pepper and Onion, the yolks of hard Eggs minced, some sweet herbs and a little salt, let these boil together half an hour or more:

Then beat it up with Butter and Limon; then dish your Meat upon Sippets, and pour it on; garnish your Dish with the hard Whites of Eggs and Parsley minced together, with sliced Limon, so serve it; thus you may dress a Leg or a Brest of Mutton if you please.

223. *To stew a Loin of Mutton.*

Cut your meat in Steaks, and put it into so much water as will cover it, when it is scummed, put to three or four Onions sliced, with some Turneps, whole Cloves, and sliced Ginger, when it is half stewed, put in sliced Bacon and some sweet herbs minced small, some Vinegar and Salt, when it is ready, put in some Capers, then dish your Meat upon Sippets and serve it in, and garnish your Dish with Barberries and Limon.

224. *To boil a Haunch of Venison.*

Boil it in water and salt, with some Coleflowers and some whole spice; then take some of the Broth, a little Mace, and a Cows Udder boiled tender and sliced thin, a little Horse-radish root searced, and a few sweet herbs; boil all these together, and put in a little Salt, when your Venison is ready, dish it, and lay your Cows Udder and the Coleflowers over it, then beat up your Sauce, and pour over it; then garnish your Dish with Limon and Parsley and Barberries, and so serve it; this Sauce is also good with a powdered Goose boiled, but first larded.

225. *To make white Broth with Meat or without.*

Take a little Mutton broth, and as much of Sack, and boil it with whole Spice, sweet herbs, Dates sliced, Currans and a little Salt, when it is enough, or very near, strain in some blanched Almonds, then thicken it with the yolks of Eggs beaten, and sweeten it with Sugar, and so serve it in with thin slices of white Bread:

Garnish with stewed Prunes, and some plumped Raisins.

This may be served in also with any meat proper for to be served with white Broth.

226. *To make good stewed Broth.*

Take a hinder Leg of Beef and a pair of Marrow Bones, boil them in a great Pot with water and a little Salt, when it boiles, and is skimmed, put in some whole Spice, and some Raisins and Currans, then put in some Manchet sliced thin, and soaked in some of the Broth, when it is almost enough, put in some stewed Prunes, then Dish your Meat, and put into your Broth a little Saffron or red Saunders, some white Wine and Sugar, so pour it over your Meat, and serve it in; Garnish your Dish with Prunes, Raisins and fine Sugar.

227. *To stew Artichokes.*

Take the bottoms of Artichokes tenderly boiled, and cut them in Quarters, stew them with white Wine, whole Spice and Marrow, with a little Salt:

When they are enough, put in Sack and Sugar, and green Plumbs preserved, so serve them; garnish the Dish with Preserves.

228. *To stew Pippins.*

Take a pound of Pippins, pare them and core them, and cut them in quarters.

Then take a pint of water and a pound of fine Sugar, and make a Syrup, and scum it, then put in your Pippins and boil them up quick, and put in a little Orange or Limon Pill very thin; when they are very clear, and their Syrup almost wasted, put in the juice of Orange and Limon, and some Butter; so serve them in upon Sippets, and strew fine Sugar about the Dish sides.

229. *To make a Sallad with fresh Salmon.*

Your Salmon being boiled and souced, mince some of it small with Apples and Onyons, put thereto Oyl, Vinegar, and Pepper; so serve it to the

Table: Garnish your Dish with Limon and Capers.

230. *To rost a Shoulder of Mutton with Oisters.*

Take a large Shoulder of Mutton, and take sweet herbs chopped small, and mixed with beaten Eggs and a little Salt, take some great Oisters, and being dried from their Liquor, dip them in these Eggs, and fry them a little, then stuff your meat well with them, then save some of them for sauce, and rost your Mutton, and baste it with Claret Wine, Butter, and Salt, save the Gravie, and put it with the Oisters into a Dish to stew with some Anchovies, and Claret Wine: when your meat is enough, rub the Dish with a Shelot, and lay your meat in it, and then put some Capers into your Sauce, and pour over it, so serve it in; Garnish your Dish with Olives, Capers, and Samphire.

231. *To rost a Calves Head with Oisters.*

Split your Calves Head as to boil, and let it lie in water a while, then wash it well, and cut out the Tongue, then boil your Head a little, also the Tongue and Brains, then mince the Brains and Tongue with a little Sage, Oisters and Marrow put amongst it when it is minced, three or four Eggs well beaten, Ginger, Pepper, Nutmeg, Grated Bread and Salt, and a little Sack, make it pretty thick, then take the Head and fill it with this, and bind it close, and spit it and rost it, and save the Gravie which comes from it in a Dish, baste it well with Butter, put to this Gravie some Oisters, and some sweet Herbs minced fine, a little white Wine, and a sliced Nutmeg; when the Head is rosted, set the Dish of Sauce upon hot Coals with some Butter and a little salt, and the Juice of an Orange, beat it up thick and Dish your Head, and serve it in with this Sauce; garnish your Dish with stewed Oisters and Barberries.

232. *Sauce for Woodcocks Snites.*

When you spit your Fowl, put in an Onion in the Belly, when it is rosted, take the Gravie of it, and some Claret Wine, and an Anchovie with a little Pepper and Salt, so serve them.

233. *To make Sauce for Partridges.*

Take grated Bread, Water and Salt, and a whole Onion boiled together, when it is well boiled, take out the Onion, and put in minced Limon, and a piece of Butter, and serve them in with it.

234. *To rost Larks with Bacon.*

When your Larks are pull'd and drawn, wash them and spit them with a thin slice of Bacon and a Sage Leaf between the Legs of every one, make your Sauce with the Juice of Oranges and a little Claret Wine, and some Butter, warm them together, and serve them up with it.

235. *To make Sauce for Quails.*

Take some Vine Leaves dried before the fire in a dish and mince them, then put some Claret Wine and a little Pepper and Salt to it, and a piece of Butter, and serve them with it.

This Sauce is also for rosted Pigeons.

236. *To rost a whole Pig without the Skin, with a Pudding in his Belly.*

Make ready the Pig for the Spit, then spit it and lay it down to the fire, and when you can take off the Skin, take it from the fire and flay it, then put such a Pudding as you love into the Belly of it, then sew it up, and stick it with Thyme and Limon Pill, and lay it down again, and rost it and bast it with Butter, and set a Dish under it to catch the Gravie, into which put a little sliced Nutmeg, and a little Vinegar, and a little Limon and some Butter; heat them together: when your Pig is enough, bread it, but first froth it up with Butter and a little Salt, then serve it in with this Sauce to the Table with the Head on.

237. *To fry Artichokes.*

Take the bottoms of Artichokes tenderly boiled, and dip them in beaten Eggs and a little Salt, and fry them with a little Mace shred among the Eggs; then take Verjuice, Butter and Sugar, and the Juice of an Orange, Dish your Artichokes, and lay on Marrow fried in Eggs to keep it whole, then lay your Sauce, or rather pour it on, and serve them in.

238. *To make Toasts of Veal.*

Take a rosted Kidney of Veal, cold and minced small, put to it grated bread, Nutmeg, Currans, Sugar and Salt, with some Almonds blanched and beaten with Rosewater, mingle all these together with beaten Eggs and a little Cream, then cut thin slices of white Bread, and lay this Compound between two of them, and so fry them, and strew Sugar on them, and serve them in.

239. *To make good Pancakes.*

Take twenty Eggs with half the Whites, and beat them well and mix them with fine flower and beaten Spice, a little Salt, Sack, Ale, and a little Yeste, do not make your Batter too thin, then beat it well, and let it stand a little while to rise, then fry them with sweet Lard or with Butter, and serve them in with the Juice of Orange and Sugar.

240. *To fry Veal.*

Cut part of a Leg of Veal into thin slices, and hack them with the back of a Knife, then season them with beaten Spice and Salt, and lard them well with Hogs Lard, then chop some sweet herbs, and beat some Eggs and mix together and dip them therein, and fry them in Butter, then stew them with a little white Wine and some Anchovies a little while, then put in some Butter, and shake them well, and serve them in with sliced Limon over them.

241. *To make good Paste.*

Take to a peck of fine flower three pound of butter, and three Eggs, and a little cold Cream, and work it well together, but do not break your Butter too small, and it will be very fine Crust, either to bake meat in, or fruit, or what else you please.

It is also a very fine Dumplin, if you make it into good big Rolls, and boil them and butter them, or roul some of it out thin, and put a great Apple therein, and boil and butter them, with Rosewater, Butter and Sugar.

242. *To make good Paste to raise.*

Take to a Peck of Flower two pounds of Butter and a little tried Suet, let them boil with a little Water or Milk, then put two Eggs into your Flower, and mix them well together, then make a hole in the middle of your Flower, and put in the top of your boiling Liquor, and so much of the rest as will make it in to a stiff Paste, then lay it into a warm Cloth to rise.

243. *Paste for cold Baked meats.*

Take to every Peck of Flower one pound of Butter or a little more, with hot Liquor as the other, and put a little dissolved Isinglass in it, because such things require strength; you may not forget Salt in all your Pastes, and work these Pastes made with hot Liquor much more than the other.

244. *To make a Veal Pie in Summer.*

Take thin slices of a Fillet of Veal, then having your Pie ready and Butter in it, lay in your Veal seasoned with a little Nutmeg and Salt so cover it with Butter, and close it and bake it, then against it be drawn, scald some Goosberries or Grapes in Sugar and water as to preserve, and when you open your Pie, put in pieces of Marrow boiled in white Wine with a little blade of Mace:

Then put these Grapes or Goosberries over all, or else some hard Lettuce or Spinage boiled and buttered.

245. *To make a Pie of Shrimps, or of Prawns.*

Pick them clean from their Shells, and have in readiness your Pie with Butter in the bottom, then lay in your Fish with some large Mace and Nutmeg, and then Butter again, and so bake it:

Then cut it up and put in some White Wine and an Anchovy or two, and some Butter, and so serve them in hot; thus you may do with Lobsters or Crabs, or with Crafish.

246. *To make a Pie of Larks, or of Sparrows.*

Pluck your Birds and draw them, then fill the Bellies of them with this mixture following, grated bread, sweet herbs minced small, Beef Suet or Marrow minced, Almonds blanched and beated with Rosewater, a little Cream; beaten Spice, and a little Salt, some Eggs and some Currans, mix these together, and do as I have said, then having your Pie ready raised or laid in your baking-pan, put in Butter, and then fill it with Birds.

Then put in Nutmeg, Pepper and Salt, and put in the yolks of hard Eggs, and some sweet herbs minced, then lay in pieces of Marrow, and cover it with Butter, and so close it and bake it; then cut it open and wring in the Juice of an Orange and some Butter, and serve it.

247. *To make a Lettuce Pie.*

Take your Cabbage Lettuce and cut them in halves, wash them and boil them in water and salt very green, then drain them from the water, so having your Pie in readiness, put in Butter; then put in your boiled Lettuce, with some Marrow, Raisins of the Sun stoned, Dates stoned and sliced thin, with some large Mace, and Nutmeg sliced, then put in more Butter, close it and bake it; then cut it open, and put in Verjuice, Butter and Sugar, and so serve it.

[Transcriber's note: no number in original] *To stew a Neck of Mutton.*

Put your Neck of Mutton cut in Steaks into so much Wine and Water as will cover it, with some whole Spice, let it stew till it be enough, then put in two Anchovies, and a handful of Capers, with a piece of sweet Butter shake it very well, and serve it upon Sippets.

248. *To make a Pie of a rosted Kidney of Veal.*

Mince the Kidney with the Fat, and put to it some sweet herbs minced very small, a quarter of a pound of Dates stoned, and sliced thin and minced, season it with beaten Spice, Sugar and Salt, put in half a pound of Currans, and some grated bread, mingle all these together very well with Verjuice and Eggs, and make them into Balls, so put some Butter into your Pie, and then these Balls, then more Butter, so close it and bake it;

Then cut it open, and put in Verjuice, Butter and Sugar made green with the Juice of some Spinage, add to it the yolks of Eggs.

249. *To make a Potato Pie.*

Having your Pie ready, lay in Butter, and then your Potatoes boiled very tender, then some whole Spice and Marrow, Dates and the yolks of hard Eggs blanched Almonds, and Pistacho Nuts, the Candied Pills of Citron, Orange and Limon, put in more Butter close it and bake it, then cut it open, and put in Wine, Sugar, the yolks of Eggs and Butter.

250. *To make a Pig Pie.*

Spit a whole Pigg and rost it till it will flay, then take it off the Spit, and take off the Skin, and lard it with Hogs Lard; season it with Pepper, Salt, Nutmeg and Sage, then lay it into your Pie upon some

Butter, then lay on some large Mace, and some more Butter, and close it and bake it: It is either good hot or cold.

251. *To make a Carp Pie.*

Take a large Carp and scale him, gut and wash him clean, and dry him well, then lay Butter into your Pie, and fill your Carps belly with this Pudding; grated bread, sweet herbs, and a little Bacon minced small, the yolks of hard Eggs and an Anchovie minced, also a little Marrow, Nutmeg, and then put in a little Salt, but a very little, and make some of this up in Balls, then Lard the Carp, sew up his Belly, and lay him into your Pie, then lay in the Balls of Pudding, with some Oysters, Shrimps and Capers, and the yolks of hard Eggs and a little Slices of Bacon, then put in large Mace and Butter, so close it and bake it, then cut off the Lid, and stick it full of pretty Conceits made in Paste, and serve it in hot.

252. *To make an Almond Tart.*

Take a Quart of Cream, and when it boils, put in half a pound of sweet Almonds blanched and beaten with Rosewater, boil them together till it be thick, always stirring it for fear it burn, then when it is cold, put in a little raw Cream, the yolks of twelve Eggs, and some beaten Spice, some Candied Citron Pill and Eringo Roots sliced, with as much fine Sugar as will sweeten it, then fill your Tart and bake it, and stick it with Almonds blanched, and some Citron Pill, and strew on some small French Comfits of several colours, and garnish your Dish with Almonds blanched, and preserved Barberries.

253. *To make a dainty White-Pot.*

Take a Manchet cut like Lozenges, and scald it in some Cream, then put to it beaten Spice, Eggs, Sugar and a little Salt, then put in Raisins, and Dates stoned, and some Marrow; do not bake it too much for fear it Whey, then strew on some fine Sugar and serve it in.

254. *To make a Red Deer Pie.*

Bone your Venison, and if it be a Side, then skin it, and beat it with an Iron Pestle but not too small, then lay it in Claret wine, and Vinegar, in some close thing two days and nights if it be Winter, else half so long, then drain it and dry it very well, and if lean, lard it with fat Bacon as big as your finger, season it very high with all manner of Spices and Salt, make your Pie with Rye Flower, round and very high, then lay store of Butter in the bottom and Bay Leaves, then lay in your Venison with more Bay leaves and Butter; so close it, and make a Tunnel in the middle, and bake it as long as you do great Loaves, when it is baked, fill it up with melted Butter, and so keep it two or three months, serve it in with the Lid off, and Bay Leaves about the Dish; eat it with mustard and sugar.

255. *To make a Pie of a Leg of Pork.*

Take a Leg of Pork well powdred and stuffed with all manner of good Herbs, and Pepper, and boil it very tender, then take off the Skin, and stick it with Cloves and Sage Leaves, then put it into your Pie with Butter top and bottom, close it and bake it, and eat it cold with Mustard and Sugar.

256. *To make a Lamprey Pie.*

Take your Lamprey and gut him, and take away the black string in the back, wash him very well, and dry him, and season him with Nutmeg, Pepper and Salt, then lay him into your Pie in pieces with Butter in the bottom, and some Shelots and Bay Leaves and more Butter, so close it and bake it, and fill it up with melted Butter, and keep it cold, and serve it in with some Mustard and Sugar.

257. *To make a Salmon Pie.*

Take a Joll of Salmon raw, and scale it and lay it into your Pie upon Butter and Bay leaves, then season it with whole spice and a little Salt, then lay on some Shrimps and Oysters with some Anchovies, then more Spice and Butter, so close the lid and bake it, but first put in some White Wine, serve it hot, then if it wants, put in more Wine and Butter.

258. *To make a Pudding of French Barley.*

Take French Barley tenderly boiled, then take to one Pint of Barley half a Manchet grated, and four Ounces of sweet Almonds blanched and beeten with Rosewater, half a Pint of Cream, and eight Eggs with half the Whites, season it with Nutmeg, Mace, Sugar and Salt, then put in some Fruit, both Raisins and Currans, and some Marrow, mingle these well together, and fill Hogs Guts with it.

259. *To make a hasty Pudding in a Bag or Cloth.*

Boil a Quart of thick Cream with six spoonfuls of fine Flower, then season it with Nutmeg and Salt, then wet a Cloth, and flower it and butter it, then boil it, and butter it, and serve it in.

260. *To make a Shaking Pudding.*

Take a Quart of Cream and boil it, then put in some Almonds blanched and beaten, when it is boiled and almost cold, put in eight Eggs, and half the Whites, with a little grated Bread, Spice and Sugar, and a very little Salt;

Then wet Flower and Butter, and put it in a Cloth and boil it, but not too much, serve it in with Rosewater, Butter and Sugar, and strew it with small French Comfits.

261. *To make a Haggus Pudding.*

Take a Calves Chaldron well scowred, boiled, and the Kernels taken out, mince it small, then take four or five Eggs, and half the Whites, some thick Cream, grated bread, Rosewater and Sugar, and a little Salt, Currans and Spice, and some sweet herbs chopped small, then put in some Marrow or Suet finely shred, so fill the Guts, and boil them.

262. *To make an Oatmeal Pudding.*

Take the biggest Oatmeal and steep it in warm Cream one night, then put in some sweet herbs minced small, the yolks of Eggs, Sugar, Spice, Rosewater and a little Salt, with some Marrow, then Butter a Cloth, and boil it well, and serve it in with Rosewater, Butter and Sugar.

263. *To make Puddings of Wine.*

Slice two Manchets into a Pint of White Wine, and let your Wine be first mulled with Spice, and with Limon Pill, then put to it ten Eggs well beaten with Rosewater, some Sugar and a little Salt, with some Marrow and Dates, so bake it a very little, strew Sugar on it, and serve it; instead of Manchet you may use Naples Bisket, which is better.

264. *To make Puddings with Hogs Lights.*

Parboil them very well, and mince them small with Suet of a Hog, then mix it with bread grated, and some Cream and Eggs, Nutmeg, Rosewater, Sugar and a little Salt, with some Currans, mingle them well together, and fill the Guts and boil them.

265. *To make Stone Cream.*

Boil a quart of Cream with whole spice then pour it out into a Dish, but let it be one quarter consumed in the boiling, then stir it till it be almost cold, then put some Runnet into it as for a Cheese, and stir it well together, and colour it with a little Saffron, serve it in with Sack and Sugar.

266. *To make a Posset Pie with Apples.*

Take the Pulp of rosted Apples and beat it well with Sugar and Rosewater to make it very sweet, then mix it with sweet Cream, and the yolks of raw Eggs, some Spice and Sack, then having your Paste ready in your Bake-pan, put in this stuff and bake it a little, then stick it with Candied Pills, and so serve it in cold.

267. *To dry Pippins about* Christmas *or before.*

When your Houshold Bread is drawn, then set in a Dish full of Pippins, and about six hours after take them out and lay them in several Dishes one by one, and flat them with your hands a little, so do twice a day, and still set them into a warm Oven every time till they are dry enough; then lay them into Boxes with Papers between every Lay.

268. *To make Snow Cream.*

Take a Quart of Cream, and 4 Ounces of blanched Almonds, beaten and strained, with half a Pint of White Wine, a piece of Orange Pill and a Nutmeg sliced, and three Sprigs of Rosemary, mix these things together, and let them stand three hours, then strain it, and put the thick part into a deep Dish, and sweeten it with Sugar, then beat some Cream with the Whites of Eggs till it be a thick Froth, and cast the Froth over it to a good thickness.

269. *To boil Whitings or Flounders.*

Boil some White Wine, Water, and Salt, with some sweet Herbs and whole Spice; when it boils put in a little Vinegar, for that will make Fish crisp, then let it boil apace and put in your Fish, and boil them till they swim, then take them out and drain them, and make Sauce for them with some of the Liquor and an Anchovie or two, some Butter and some Capers, heat them over the Fire, and beat it up thick and pour it over them; garnish your Dish with Capers and Parsley, Oranges and Limons and let it be very hot when you serve it in.

270. *To make a Pie of a Gammon of Bacon.*

Take a *Westphalia* Gammon, and boil it tender with hay in the Kettle, then take off the Skin and stick it with Cloves and strew it with Pepper, then make your Pie ready, and put it therein with Butter at the bottom, then cover your Bacon with Oysters, parboiled in Wine and their own Liquor, and put in Balls made of Sausage meat, then put in the Liquor of the parboiled Oysters, some whole Spice and Bay Leaves, with some Butter, so close it, and bake it and eat it cold, you may put into it the yolks of hard Eggs if you please, serve it with Mustard Sugar and Bay Leaves.

271. *To bake a Bulloks Cheek to be eaten hot.*

Take your Cheek and stuff it very well with Parsley and sweet herbs chopped, then put it into a Pot with some Claret wine and a little strong Beer, and some whole Spice, and so season it well with Salt to your taste, and cover your Pot and bake it, then take it out, and pull out the Bones, and serve it upon tosted bread with some of the Liquor.

272. *To bake a Bullocks Cheek to eat cold, as Venison.*

Take a Bullocks Cheek, or rather two fair fat Cheeks, and lay them in water one night, then take out every bone, and stuff it very well with all manner of Spice and Salt, then put it into a Pot, one Cheek clapped close together upon the other, then lay it over with Bay Leaves, and put in a Quart of Claret Wine, so cover the Pot and bake it with Houshold Bread, when you draw it, pour all the Liquor out, and take only the fat of it and some melted Butter, and pour in again, serve it cold with Mustard and Sugar, and dress it with Bay Leaves, it will eat like Venison.

273. *To make a Bacon Froize.*

Take eight Eggs well beaten, and a little Cream, and a little Flower, and beat them well together to be like other Batter, then fry very thin slices of Bacon, and pour some of this over, then fry it, and turn the other side, and pour more upon that, so fry it and serve it to the Table.

274. *To make fryed Nuts.*

Take Eggs, Flower, Spice and Cream, and make it into a Paste, then make it into round Balls and fry them, they must be as big as Walnuts, be sure to shake them well in the Pan and fry them brown, then roul some out thin, and cut them into several shapes, and fry them, so mix them together, and serve them in with Spice beaten and Sugar.

275. *To make a* Sussex *Pancake.*

Take only some very good Pie Paste made with hot Liquor, and roul it thin, and fry it with Butter, and serve it in with beaten spice and sugar as hot as you can.

276. *To make a Venison Pasty.*

Take a Peck of fine Flower, and three Pounds of fresh Butter, break your Butter into your Flower, and put in one Egg, and make it into a Past with so much cold cream as you think fit, but do not mould it too much, then roul it pretty thin and broad, almost square, then lay some Butter on the bottom, then season your Venison on the fleshy side with Pepper grosly beaten, and Salt mixed, then lay your Venison upon your butter with the seasoned side downward, and then cut the Venison over with your Knife quite cross the Pasty to let the Gravie come out the better in baking, then rub some seasoning in those Cuts, and do not lay any else because it will make it look ill-favoured and black, then put some paste rouled thin about the Meat to keep it in compass, and lay Butter on the top, then close it up and bake it very well, but you must trim it up with several Fancies made in the same Paste, and make also a Tunnel or Vent, and just when you are going to set it into the Oven, put in half a Pint of Clarret Wine, that will season your

Venison finely, and make it shall not look or taste greasie, thus you may bake Mutton if you please.

277. *To make a brave Tart of several Sweet Meats.*

Take some Puff-paste, and roule it very thin, and lay it in the bottom of your baking-pan, then lay in a Lay of preserved Rasberries, then some more Paste very thin to cover them, then some Currans preserved, and then a Sheet of Paste to cover them, then Cherries, and another Sheet to cover them, then any white Sweet-Meat, as Pippins, white Plumbs or Grapes, so lid it with Puff-paste, cut in some pretty Fancy to shew the Fruit, then bake it, and stick it full of Candied Pills, and serve it in cold.

278. *To make Ice and Snow.*

Take new Milk and some Cream and mix it together, and put it into a Dish, and set it together with Runnet as for a Cheese, and stir it together, when it is come, pour over it some Sack and Sugar, then take a Pint of Cream and a little Rosewater, and the Whites of three Eggs, and whip it to a froth with a Birchen Rod, then as the Froth arises, cast it upon your Cream which hath the Runnet in it, till it lies deep, then lay on Bunches of preserved Barberries here and there carelesly, and cast more Snow upon them, which will look exceeding well; then garnish your Dish being broad brim'd with all kind of Jellies in pretty-fancies, and several Colours.

279. *To make a Mutton Pie.*

Cut a Loin or Neck of Mutton in steaks, and season it with Pepper and Salt, and Nutmeg, then lay it in your Pie upon Butter; then fill up your

Pie with Apples sliced thin, and a few great Onions sliced thin, then put in more Butter, and close it and bake it, and serve it in hot.

280. *To poach Eggs the best way.*

Boil Vinegar and Water together with a few Cloves and Mace, when it boiles break in your Eggs, and turn them about gently with a Tin slice till the White be hard, then take them up, and pare away what is not handsom, and lay them on Sippets, and strew them over with plumped Currans, then take Verjuice, Butter and Sugar heat together, and pour over, and serve them in hot.

281. *A good Sallad in Winter.*

Take a good hard Cabbage, and with a sharp Knife shave it so thin as you may not discern what it is, then serve it with Oil and Vinegar.

282. *Another Sallad in Winter.*

Take Corn Sallad clean picked and also well washed, and clear from the water, put it into a Dish in some handsom form with some Horse Radish scraped, and some Oil and Vinegar.

283. *To make Sorrel Sopps for Green Geese or Chickens, or for a Sick Body to eat alone.*

Take a good quantity of French Sorrel clean picked, and stamp it in a Mortar, then strain it into a Dish, and set it over a Chafing dish of Coals, and put a little Vinegar to it, then when it is thick by wasting, wring in the

Juice of a Limon and sweeten it with Sugar, and put in a little grated bread and Nutmeg, then warm another Dish with thin slices of white bread, and put some butter to your Sorrel Liquor, and pour over them, serve them in with Slices of Limon and fine Sugar.

284. *To make Green Sauce for a powdred Leg of Pork, or for a Spring.*

Take a great quantity of French Sorrel, and pick out the Strings and wash it well, and drain it clean from the water, then stamp it in a Mortar till it be extream fine, then put in grated bread and beat it again, then a few Currans and the yolks of hard Eggs, and when it is beaten to a kind of Pap, put in a little Vinegar and Sugar into it; so serve it in upon a Plate with your Meat.

285. *To make* Vin de Molosso, *or Treacle Wine.*

Take fair Water and make it so strong with Molossoes, otherwise called Treacle, as that it will bear an Egg, then boil it with a Bag of all kinds of Spices, and a Branch or two of Rosemary, boil it and scum it, and put in some sweet herbs or flowers, according to the time of the year, boil it till a good part be consumed, and that it be very clear, then set it to cool in several things, and when it is almost cold, work it with yest, as you do Beer, the next day put it into the Vessel, and so soon as it hath done working stop it up close, and when it hath stood a fortnight, bottle it, this is a very wholesom Drink against any Infection, or for any that are troubled with the Ptisick.

286. *For a Consumption, an excellent Medicine.*

Take Shell Snails, and cast Salt upon them, and when you think they are cleansed well from their slime, wash them, and crack their Shells and take them off, then wash them in the distilled Water of Hysop, then put them into a Bag made of Canvas, with some white Sugar Candy beaten, and hang up the Bag, and let it drop as long as it will, which if you bruise the Snails before you hang them up, it is the better; this Liquor taken morning and evening a Spoonful at a time is very rare.

287. *A Suitable Dish for Lent.*

Take a large Dish with broad Brims, and in the middle put blanched Almonds round about them, Raisins of the Sun, and round them Figs, and beyond them all coloured Jellies, and on the Brims Fig-Cheese.

288. *To make a Rock in Sweet-Meats.*

First take a flat broad voiding Basket, then have in readiness a good thick Plum Cake, then cut your Cake fit to the bottom of the Basket, and cut a hole in the middle of it, that the foot of your Glass may go in, which must be a Fountain-Glass, let it be as high a one as you can get; put the foot of it in the hole of the Cake edgling that it may stand the faster, then tie the Cake fast with a Tape to the Basket, first cross one way and then another, then tie the foot of the Glass in that manner too, that it may stand steady, then cut some odd holes in your Cake carelesly, then take some Gum Dragon steeped in Rosewater, and mix it with some fine Sugar, not too thick, and with that you must fasten all your Rock together, in these holes which you cut in your Cake you must fasten some sort of Biskets, as Naples Biskets, and other common Bisket made long, and some ragged, and some coloured, that they may look like great ill-favoured, Stones, and some handsome, some long, some short, some bigger, and some lesser, as you know Nature doth afford, and some of one colour and some of another, let some stand upright and some aslannt, and some quite along, and fasten them all with your Gum, then put in some better Sweet-meats, as Mackeroons and Marchpanes, carelesly made as to the shape, and not put on the Rock in a set form, also some rough Almond Cakes made with the long slices of Almonds (as I have directed before;) so build it up in this manner, and fasten it with the Gum and Sugar, till it be very high, then in some places you must put whole Quinces Candied, both red and white, whole Orange Pills and Limon Pills Candied; dried Apricocks, Pears and Pippins Candied, whole Peaches Candied, then set up here and there great lumps of brown and white Sugar-candy upon the stick, which much resembles some clusters of fine Stones growing on a Rock; for Sand which lies sometimes among the little Stones, strew some brown Sugar; for Moss, take herbs of a Rock Candy; then you must make the likeness of Snakes and Snails and Worms, and of any venomous Creature you can think of; make them in Sugar Plate and colour them to their likeness, and put them in the holes that they may seem to lurk, and some Snails creeping one way and some other; then take all manner of Comfits, both rough and smooth, both great and small, and colour many of them, some of one colour and some of another, let some be white and some speckled, then when you have coloured them, and that they are dry, mix them together and throw them into the Clefts, but not too many in one place, for that will hide the shape of your work, then throw in some Chips of all sorts of Fruit Candied, as Orange, Limon, Citron, Quince, Pear, and Apples, for of all these you may make Chips; then all manner of dryed Plumbs, and Cherries, Cornelions dryed, Rasps and Currans; and in some places throw a few Prunelles, Pistacho Nuts, blanched Almonds, Pine Kernels, or any such like, and a pound of the great round perfumed Comfits; then take the lid off the top of the Glass and fill it with preserved Grapes, and fill another with some Harts-horn Jelly, place these two far from one another, and if you set some kind of Fowl, made in Marchpanes,

www.ingramcontent.com/pod-product-compliance
Lightning Source LLC
Chambersburg PA
CBHW081624100526

44590CB00021B/3582